Angels
Watching
OVER YOU

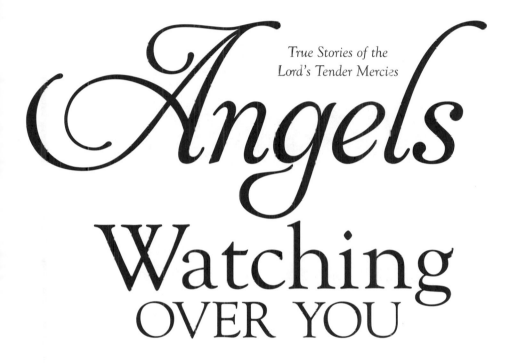

True Stories of the
Lord's Tender Mercies

Angels

Watching
OVER YOU

JUDY C. OLSEN

Covenant Communications, Inc.

Covenant

Cover image: *Butterfly on Flower* © Patricia Ramos

Cover design copyright © 2013 by Covenant Communications, Inc.

Published by Covenant Communications, Inc.
American Fork, Utah

Printed in the United States of America
First Printing: February 2013

19 18 17 16 15 14 13   10 9 8 7 6 5 4 3 2 1

ISBN 978-1-62108-327-6

To my wonderful extended family who carry on the righteous
traditions of their parents

Acknowledgments

I owe a sincere thank you to all of the people who have opened their hearts and shared very personal and meaningful chapters of their lives through the pages of this book. In every story, someone has felt the hand of the Lord guiding them, responding to their deepest desires, or protecting them. These stories combine in a powerful testament that Jesus lives, hears our prayers, and is aware of each of us. Thank you for sharing.

Introduction

Brigham Young once said, "There is no doubt, if a person lives according to the revelations given to God's people, he may have the Spirit of the Lord to signify to him his will, and to guide and to direct him in the discharge of his duties, in his temporal as well as his spiritual exercises. I am satisfied, however, that in this respect, we live far beneath our privileges" (Brigham Young. *Discourses of Brigham Young*, comp. by John A. Widtsoe, 1943, 32).

As Latter-day Saints grow in faith, testimony, and righteousness, they will begin to experience ever greater spiritual "privileges," such as comfort, protection, and guidance from the Spirit. The Lord's tender mercies are abundant, even when we do not receive desired outcomes or blessings. He is always mindful of us and is watching over us.

Ministrations from beyond the veil come under the direction of the Savior through the power of the Holy Ghost, and this help can take many forms, from a simple thought to direct answers to prayer to actual intervention from the other side in times of danger or difficulty. There is help from angels watching over us. And sometimes, there are even miracles waiting for those in greatest need.

—Judy Olsen

Table of Contents

He Takes Us Where We Need to Be

*And behold, I tell you these things that ye may learn wisdom;
that ye may learn that when ye are in the service of your fellow
beings ye are only in the service of your God.*

—*Mosiah 2:17*

An Answer to Prayer

By Jan Hitchcock

Roslyn had been my visiting teacher for at least a year and had never missed seeing me at least once a month. Sometimes she just brought a treat to my door and inquired about the family, but usually she made a regular visit that included a lesson. She had seven children, including one handicapped child, so in spite of her faithful attention to me, I always felt she was too busy and under too much pressure for me to call her if I had a problem.

That year my life changed drastically. My daughter returned home to live with my husband and me. She had two small children, ages two and three, and she was expecting a baby in five months. Those five months were fraught with problems. Both of her children got pneumonia, and so did my daughter. The doctor didn't want her to cough too much because the hard coughing could cause the uterus to rupture, so he kept her sedated a lot of the time. She was also in constant undiagnosed pain, which we later learned was fibromyalgia, and on top of all of that, she was allergic to the baby and had hives over most of her body.

On many occasions during those five months, I stood at her bedroom door as she slept and wondered how I could take care of her children if she died and how I could possibly bear the sorrow of her loss. When I told my daughter my fears about her not surviving this pregnancy, she said she had been thinking the same thing, and we discussed plans for her children's future if something happened to her.

Five months later, she gave birth to a healthy baby boy by cesarean section, and some of her problems began to resolve. Since I was the sole caretaker of her two other children, I had to be at home on this special day. Yet I longed to be with her—I *needed* to be with her. She had suffered so much, and now there was hope at last for her recovery. I felt we should be sharing this moment together. And as any grandmother will attest, I also wanted to welcome my newest grandson into the world.

I began calling family, friends, and ward members early in the morning after the baby's birth. After calling everyone I thought might be able to help, I began to despair. It seemed that no one was available, but each one had good reasons why they couldn't help that particular day. I didn't even call Roslyn because I knew how busy she was, and I knew she would feel guilty if I asked her and she couldn't help. Finally, I bowed my head and offered a heartfelt prayer to my Father in Heaven that I would know whom I could call for help that day.

Within seconds of ending my prayer, my phone rang. It was my visiting teacher, Roslyn. In her cheerful voice, she said, "Hi, Jan, do you need some help with your grandkids today?" I couldn't believe my prayer could be answered so quickly. She said she wasn't really doing anything that day, all her children were in school, and she just *thought of me and wondered if she could be of help.* She not only helped that day but several more times until my daughter came home from the hospital.

My patriarchal blessing says that the "Lord is mindful of His children, and when they are striving to do that which is right, He will sustain them and make them equal to every emergency." I felt like the Lord helped me out in this emergency.

I am so thankful for those people in my life who listen and respond to promptings from the Spirit. Sister Julie B. Beck, former general president of the Relief Society, once said, "A sister in this Church has no other responsibility outside of her family that has the potential to do as much good as does visiting teaching" ("Relief Society: A Sacred Work," *Ensign,* Nov. 2009).

Roslyn offered help on a day when it meant everything to me to be by the bedside of my daughter and share the relief of her survival, as well as the joy and wonder of having brought a new baby into the world amid great personal hardship. And I am grateful that the Lord understood the righteous desires of my heart that day and opened a door for me to be where I most needed to be.

Jan Hitchcock is a mother of four grown children; is a grandmother of thirteen; and has been married to her husband, Jerry, for fifty years. She lives in Sandy, Utah, and serves as an ordinance worker in the Draper Utah Temple. Jan loves reading and belongs to two book clubs. She enjoys gardening, spending time with friends and family, singing, sewing, and writing. Last year she wrote a program for her fiftieth high school class reunion, and this year she wrote a program for her husband's family reunion. She recently took up playing the clarinet.

*And while I was thus struggling in the spirit, behold,
the voice of the Lord came into my mind.*

—*Enos 1:10*

He Knew My Heart

By Lon Pearson

Worthy fathers who hold the priesthood are promised inspiration and guidance in rearing their families. My wife, Janet, and I had both felt impressions concerning many of our decisions regarding our education, our children, employment, moves, and countless other things that came up in our lives. We had counseled together, prayed, and experienced feelings that helped us rear our five children in our home in Missouri. Still, although I'd often felt good about decisions or received spiritual feelings, I had never experienced a straightforward message meant just for me.

Until one night in March 1983.

Three years earlier I received an invitation to go to Mexico as an exchange professor for a year. I'd spent much of my professional life teaching and speaking Spanish and Portuguese, often traveling to South America. So this opportunity to live in Mexico for a year with my family excited me. I could envision all of us learning to communicate well in Spanish. I especially hoped that my oldest son, Russell, who was then in high school, would be called to a Spanish-speaking mission when he turned nineteen. That would give us a deep and special bond, and our time in Mexico would be a great preparation for such a call.

We did have a number of concerns about the children, schools, language, and so on, but we felt overall it might be a good experience for the family. Then, during our visit to the campus in Monterrey in January, the administration found out I was a member of The Church of Jesus Christ of Latter-day Saints. The invitation was immediately cancelled. I was deeply disappointed.

Two years later, in March, I received an invitation to bring my family from our home in Missouri to Utah, where I would be working as a visiting professor at Brigham Young University for the academic year of 1982–83. Suddenly, we saw the cancellation of the Mexico trip as a blessing for our family as we were able to accept the offer to teach at BYU in the Department of Spanish and Portuguese.

One day our children asked, "How far away will we have to go for stake conference?" When we told them we could probably walk to conference, they couldn't believe it. In Missouri, we traveled a hundred miles to attend conference.

Russell had not been planning to move with us to Provo. Instead, he hoped to play basketball at a small college. Yet because BYU had promised that we could have half tuition for Russell as a student, we strongly encouraged him to begin his freshman year at BYU. He soon agreed to do it.

He played soccer on the BYU junior varsity team, which I coached, and he also tried out for the junior varsity basketball team, making it to the final cuts. Since BYU is a major university, he knew he had done well to get to that point.

The school year began, and my son and I commuted from American Fork to campus—sometimes on motorcycle—allowing a bond of father-son trust and love to develop. We were assigned as home teachers, and Russell and I soon found out that we could carry out our home teaching by walking around the block! During that year, in many ways, Russell and I shared an increasingly close relationship.

In my heart, I continued to hope that Russell would be called to a Spanish-speaking mission, which would add an additional joy to our growing bond. Russell had taken Latin in high school and had enrolled in a Spanish class at BYU. This bolstered my hopes that he might follow the path that I had taken.

In preparation for his nineteenth birthday on June fifth, Russ submitted the necessary application to serve a full-time mission. He had been ordained an elder that spring.

We waited in anticipation for his call to arrive. Early one morning, about a week before it came, I awoke with a clear certainty that Russell would be called to serve in Japan. Later that morning, I shared my experience with my wife. Yet I wondered . . . could that possibly be? With all of his preparation in Latin and Spanish? But I could not doubt that I had heard the truth.

The week the official mission call arrived, Janet and I traveled to Phoenix to a professional conference. Janet took the phone call from Russell while I was out of the room. She immediately came to find me. "Russell called, and he has just received his mission call. Guess where he's going."

So strong had been my desire that he serve somewhere in Latin America that I found myself saying, "Brazil?"

Janet countered quickly: "Oh ye of little faith! He has been called to the Japan Tokyo North Mission!"

Her words settled over me with a complete understanding of the correctness of his call. Why had I said Brazil? I had known through the Spirit that he would go to Japan. I realized that the Lord, who understood my heart, had given me my own witness to help me accept my son's call with joy. My heart yielded completely in that moment. Later, as I counted back the days, I realized that this witness came to me likely at about the same time the missionary committee had made the assignment.

I know now in a deeper and more personal way that the Lord does inspire the committee of general authorities to call the individual or couple to the optimum place for both the missionary and the Lord in His work.

* * *

Nearly twenty-eight years after Russell's mission call, his oldest son, Taylor, was expecting a mission call. Russell called us with the news, asking: "Where do you think Taylor has been called to serve?"

I hesitated only a moment. "Japan."

Russ replied, "You're right. He's been called to the Japan Kobe Mission."

My son and grandson don't speak Spanish or Portuguese, but they enjoy sharing Japanese in letters and a few phone calls. And we all share in common our missionary service for the Lord. In the end, the joy of that service—in whatever language—binds us together.

After raising five children over five decades of marriage spent in California, Missouri, Maryland, and Nebraska, Lon and Janet Pearson have settled in Utah. Lon, recently retired as a professor of Spanish, has served twice as a bishop. He and Janet served missions in Mexico and Chile. Currently, they work in the Draper Utah Temple. They enjoy traveling to Canada, Missouri, and points in between to visit their twenty-one grandchildren.

Be thou humble; and the Lord thy God shall lead thee by the hand, and give thee answer to thy prayers.

—D&C 112:10

Preparing for . . . What?

By Debora Escalante

February 1, 1995, was the beginning of my single-parenthood journey with my five children, ages three to twelve. Due to a stake reorganization, it was also my first week attending a new ward. In only one week's time, we had changed from heading down the "ideal" Mormon family path in one ward to being perhaps the only "broken" family in another.

But I had other things to worry about. It soon became apparent that I would need to be the primary financial provider for the family, and even though I had a master's degree in children's theatre, I felt the need to prepare myself to find a job that would work well with both raising children and attending graduate school again. I began praying for guidance regarding what kind of employment would work out best while I attended classes.

Within a week, a neighbor from the old ward called to ask me if I would be interested in a part-time position as the teacher of the gifted and talented students at the local elementary school. It sounded interesting, but there was one hitch: the principal was planning to hire within the next thirty minutes. It was Friday afternoon, and I would need to dash over for an interview within that time.

I felt too rushed to get over there in that short time frame, so I thanked her for thinking of me and suggested they go ahead and make their selection from among the candidates who had already applied. She graciously accepted my refusal, saying that she understood my concern about the short notice.

Almost immediately after hanging up, I regretted my decision, and I continued to regret it all weekend. A part-time job at the nearby school would have worked well with my children's schedule as well as my own.

Monday morning, the phone rang, and a woman identified herself as the assistant principal of the school and said, "I don't know you, but you have a major cheering squad here, and we are wondering if you would reconsider and come talk with us about the position."

Relief flooded over me. I interviewed and got the job. And I recognized the opportunity the Lord had provided for me—He *was* listening to and answering my prayers.

At the end of the school year, the assistant principal offered me a full-time position at another school, but it included an afterschool program that would leave my children home alone until evening, and as much as I needed full-time work, the sacrifice seemed too great.

About that time, a woman I had recently met at church called me to ask if I had ever considered becoming a school librarian. I definitely had not. She told me about the need for a librarian at her school and gave me the information I would need to apply for the position. I thanked her, but again, I had no intention of applying.

She called again a few days later to ask if I had applied, and I had to confess that I hadn't. This time she explained that the position would be closing the following afternoon at four p.m. and that I should apply now, even if I wasn't sure if I was interested. So at three fifty p.m. the following afternoon, I walked into the district employment office and filled out the application. I really hadn't intended to work in K–12 education!

I didn't hear anything from the school for a few days and thought I wouldn't have to worry about the position, but on Monday of the following week, the principal called and asked me to come in for an interview. I was offered the position, and it was based on a traditional contract at a year-round school—a contract that made it possible to attend graduate school at Utah State University, seventy-two miles away, two days a week. And I would get to read and tell stories to children all day—something I loved.

I eventually transferred my three youngest children to my school, not only for the innovative educational practices there but also to be able to stay close to them and their teachers. The woman—now a good friend—who had called me about the position also worked at the school, and she was able to provide transportation for my children on the days I commuted to Logan.

The Lord was definitely pointing me in a new direction.

It took me over a year to get the courage to apply to graduate school, but during that time, the elementary school where I worked served as the district professional development center for research on the human brain and learning. Because the program took place at my facility, I was able to participate in the training. Over the months that I attended those classes, I became interested in the research, which strongly influenced my choice for graduate study. I was accepted into the Instructional Technology program at USU and planned to research and develop a model for mapping and designing integrated curricula based on current brain research.

Many miracles, large and small, occurred during the next few years, and I felt like I was going in the direction the Lord wanted me to go. A number of the teachers at the elementary school were implementing my ideas and providing feedback. I had found a professor to serve as my dissertation committee chair, and he was very excited about my research topic and had the expertise and reputation to give my work guidance and credibility.

I had finished most of my coursework and was about to focus on researching and writing my dissertation when I experienced yet another change in direction—and this one came as a pretty big blow to my plans. My chair was asked to spend eighteen months at BYU–Hawaii developing online instruction and was leaving USU!

I began my search for a new chair and looked to another professor with whom I had worked on a number of projects, one of which was a study for the Utah State Office of Education. He said he was willing to be my chair; he was less enthusiastic about my research topic, but he said he would try to be supportive anyway.

I continued to move forward, but a short time later, he approached me with a new idea. By this time, I was working nearly full-time on a project at USU. He informed me there was funding available for research related to the project for the State Office of Education—if I were to change the focus of my dissertation research. Reluctantly, I once again changed direction.

My new research topic required that I meet fairly regularly with state and district public education administrators and deans of the colleges of education from all of the universities in the state. As we met, they would share their concerns and insights about the data I was gathering and provide guidance for the direction of the study. During the final year of the study, a few of the deans casually suggested that I apply to their programs upon graduation.

As I approached graduation, I decided to see if they were serious and contacted Dean Young in the McKay School of Education at Brigham Young University. Amazingly, he offered me a position working with an endowment-funded project to help elementary teachers improve their teaching through art integration. The position allowed me to integrate both my theatre and academic backgrounds.

I moved my family to Orem, just a few miles from Brigham Young University, and went to work. I loved my new position.

Three years later, due to a university restructuring and hiring freeze, I was informed that my position was in jeopardy. Yes, I worked at BYU for the School of Education; however, I was actually an employee of a BYU–public-school partnership. Most of us working under the partnership would be let go. Only a few would be retained and become BYU employees.

I couldn't imagine that the Lord would bring me to Orem and BYU only for me to become unemployed, so I remained positive and prayerful. One day as I was studying the Doctrine and Covenants, I opened to section 127, and my eyes fell on verse two: "But nevertheless, deep water is what I am wont to swim in. It all has become a second nature to me; and I feel, like Paul, to glory in tribulation."

A few days later, during my scripture study, I again opened the Doctrine and Covenants randomly, and once again, it fell on the same scripture. After it happened a third time, I started to get nervous and felt a deep sense of foreboding—until the day I decided to read a little further: "For to this day has the God of my fathers delivered me out of them all, and will deliver me from henceforth. . . . And let your diligence, and your perseverance, and patience, and your works be redoubled, and you shall in nowise lose your reward, saith the Lord of Hosts" (D&C 127:2, 4).

The contract year was approaching, and I had no promise of a job, but both the dean and assistant dean were hopeful that my position would be retained. One day I received a call from the School of Education at Utah Valley University, located only a few miles from my home, about a position in their new master's program. As usual, the position would be closing in just a few days.

I had not considered moving to a new university, and as I read the job description, I felt that my background was not a match. But I had learned over time that when the Lord opens a door, I should pay attention, so I applied for the position—once again submitting my application within hours of the deadline. When I didn't hear from them, I assumed they agreed with my thoughts about the mismatch.

It was nearly a week later when I received a call from the department chair, who apologized for taking so long to contact me for an interview. Two days and a few interviews later, I was offered a tenure-track position, teaching not only graduate courses but also undergraduate courses in elementary arts integration.

It was only after accepting the position that I realized that from the moment I first accepted the position as an elementary school librarian, I had been working for the Utah state education system in one way or another, and I had already accrued fourteen years toward a full retirement—years I would have lost if I had stayed at BYU. In addition, I now had two children attending UVU who would benefit from my employment.

I also realized that if I had pursued the original idea for my dissertation research, I would very likely be unemployed. Each change in the direction of my path led to the experience needed to move forward successfully.

I can bear a strong witness that the Lord knows our talents and abilities, and if we are willing to be led along step-by-step, He will eventually take us to the best place to use those abilities. He watches over us, and He cares very much. Often during those years, I assumed I was walking down one road to a certain destination only to find out it was merely a segment in a longer journey. Yet at every step, the Lord further prepared me for the place where I could eventually best use my skills and talents.

As much as I had enjoyed my former employments, I could only rejoice at the security and fulfillment I obtained by learning to respond to the Spirit's guidance. I am grateful for the hand of the Lord that led me along, step by step, to where I needed to be.

Debora Tholen Escalante lives in Orem, Utah, and teaches in the School of Education at Utah Valley University. She has three sons, two daughters, two daughters-in-law, one son-in-law, and three grandchildren. She loves the arts, nature, reading, and family.

Yea, and how is it that ye have forgotten that the Lord is able to do all things according to his will, for the children of men, if it so be that they exercise faith in him? Wherefore, let us be faithful to him.

—*1 Nephi 7:12*

Choosing to Believe

By Heather Clark

I have always wanted to be a mother. Since I was a little girl learning from the example of my own mother, temple marriage and motherhood have been my highest goals. They are what we're taught, what we plan and hope for. I looked forward eagerly to building an eternal family with my husband and children.

Cody and I were married in 2003, and in 2004, our daughter Elinor was born—a miracle. Meeting our perfect daughter, sent straight to us from Heavenly Father, was an experience I have no adequate words to describe. It was the closest I've ever felt to God. Watching her young body and mind grow lifted me every day. I felt like for the first time in my life, I really understood my own purpose. Motherhood helped me understand and value my physical body and my spiritual journey on earth, and it continues to be the most difficult, rewarding, heart-wrenching, joyful experience of my life.

I was twenty-seven when Elinor was born, and we didn't want to let my childbearing years slip away from us, so when Elinor was nine months old, we began trying to have another baby—eager to meet our next little one.

But as the months wore on and I couldn't conceive another child, I started to worry about infertility. We prayed and fasted. And waited.

Finally, Cody gave me a priesthood blessing in which I was promised that within one year I would give birth to a healthy baby. It was an amazing and specific promise. It was November, and I was both excited and nervous as I looked forward to this precious gift.

Two and a half months later, I had not become pregnant, and it became really hard to hold on to my faith. I wanted to believe, but I began to doubt that the promise could really be fulfilled. It was hard to keep hoping and praying for the blessing as the deadline approached.

Finally, I decided to seek medical help for my infertility. However, on my way to the clinic, I felt prompted that I should take one more pregnancy test. I felt a powerful impression of peace from the Holy Ghost, assuring me that even though the former tests had been negative, I was pregnant and everything would be okay.

I returned home, and the test was positive! I can remember few moments of such joy and elation in my life. I would give birth two weeks before the end of November. God had kept His promise, and I was going to have another child.

At my eight-week appointment, my obstetrician expressed concern about the pregnancy. But I knew the Lord's promise to me, so I sought and received multiple priesthood blessings, each promising me that I would carry our baby to term and give birth to a healthy child.

As blood work and an ultrasound followed, our fears deepened. I wanted desperately to have faith in the promises I had been given, but I was so confused and worried. What should I believe about the blessings I had received when medical science was telling me that I would lose this baby?

At eleven weeks, I miscarried. The baby we had hoped for and loved already would not be joining our family. I was confused, sorrowful, and filled with questions. Why hadn't my priesthood blessings been fulfilled? Hadn't the words of the blessings been inspired? Was my faith too weak? Were we unworthy in some way?

As challenging as these thoughts were, some questions I asked myself were even more frightening. Was the gospel true? Was priesthood power real? Did God exist, or were the things I'd believed my whole life a fantasy?

A few weeks after the miscarriage, my daughter, Elinor, became ill. Her high fever caused her to twitch and shake as her body battled the infection. I spent hours one night watching her sleep, filled with apprehension. What would stop God from taking her too? Cody gave her a blessing, promising that she would be made whole, but his words offered me no comfort. For the first time in my life, I had trouble believing in a God who really keeps His promises. Or maybe I only doubted myself. My struggling faith felt too weak to merit blessings for our family.

As I lay on the bed, watching over our daughter, I poured out my doubt and fear to my husband. Cody comforted me. "It's okay, Heather. I have faith enough for both of us."

It was enough, for the moment. I let his words carry me.

During the months that followed, Nephi's words to his rebellious and doubting brothers became a motto for me: "Yea, and how is it that ye have forgotten that the Lord is able to do all things according to his will, for the children of men, if it so be that they exercise faith in him? Wherefore, let us be faithful to him" (1 Nephi 7:12).

The difference in Nephi's word choice between *faith* and *faithful* gave me what I needed to carry on. The scripture promised that the Lord can do all things if we exercise faith. If faith was a feeling, mine was weak. I wanted to feel more, but something had closed down inside of me. Fear and doubt kept me from believing with an open heart.

It was then that I realized faith is a choice—that even while filled with uncertainty, I could choose to follow Nephi's counsel to *be faithful* to God. I decided to carry on *as though* my faith were whole, hoping and praying for the feelings of confidence and testimony to return.

Months passed, and instead of doors opening to us, I felt them closing. For example, when I was about to start fertility medication, I felt a strong prompting that this was not what I should do. *What? Why not?* Didn't God trust that I could be a good mother? In some ways, I felt rejected by God. If His power was real, why didn't He keep His promises?

Despite moments when I felt the Spirit, underlying doubt and discouragement weighed me down. There was so much fear in the possibility that everything I had grown up believing might be just a soothing fantasy.

During this time, I kept to my resolve to *be faithful*. I served in the Church. I fulfilled my callings. I went to the temple. I took the sacrament. I did my visiting teaching. I had family and personal prayer. I *chose* to be faithful to God, believing that no matter what, my life would be more joyful if I lived the principles of the gospel.

In November, around the time that our sweet baby would have been born, Cody and I went to the temple together. As usual, the questions in my heart weighed heavily on my mind. An unusually busy temple day meant that some of the women had to be seated with some of the men in the session, and I was able to sit next to my husband, giving us an unexpected opportunity to share a time of spiritual closeness. The Spirit I felt brought me so much peace.

Toward the end of the session, a temple worker prayed that those who had come to the temple seeking answers would receive those answers *today*. His words hit me with power and clarity, and I felt the warm presence of the Holy Ghost with me. I suddenly knew the Lord had answers for *me* that very day.

At the conclusion of the session, we sat quietly, waiting. Sitting very still, holding Cody's hand, I began to pray to ask the Lord for the answers I felt sure He would give me.

What followed was one of the most clear and undeniable answers I have ever received in my life. The impression came to my mind that Cody and I were to try to adopt a baby right away through LDS Family Services. As the promptings came, peace and stillness flowed over me.

I knew without a doubt that Heavenly Father was guiding me, and I felt sure of what He wanted me to do. Sitting so close to Cody, I was able to whisper my promptings to him. And he too knew that it was right. There was no hesitation. We knew clearly what the Lord wanted us to do.

Along with promptings and peace, I also received the priceless gift of healing. In the temple that day, in those few moments of quiet, the Lord healed my heart from the pain and doubt of the past year. I knew that we had not lost the baby through any lack of faith on our part, that the Lord loved us perfectly, and that He was real. I suddenly knew that all the things that we had been through in the past year were for our good and that Heavenly Father was holding our small family in His loving hands.

Two years passed after that spiritual moment in the temple. No one chose us to adopt their baby. I did not become pregnant. I didn't understand what was happening, why we were still waiting. But though there were moments of discouragement, I never fell back into the darkness where I could no longer trust the Lord. I knew that we had done what He wanted us to do, and the rest was in His hands. I had been healed of my sorrow and despair in the temple that day, and as a result, I was able to wait for the Lord to reveal His purposes.

I believed again with a whole heart that the Lord lives, loves us, and will give us what we need, even if we don't comprehend it at the time. Perhaps the Lord just needed to teach us to exercise more faith and trust in Him as we participated in a process that was costly in time, money, and emotion, without having any control over the outcome.

In the end, I believe the Lord wanted to bring me joy in the midst of trial. The gift of hope I received when I initiated adoption proceedings lifted my heart and made the waiting bearable. I felt sustained and filled with a sense of purpose and peace as we waited until the Lord's timing was right to send us another child. Adoption never worked out for us. I may never understand exactly why we were prompted to adopt, but I have learned to trust the Lord. I know He knows why, and that is enough.

In April 2009, more than two and a half years after our experience in the temple, I felt prompted to start fertility medication immediately. The direction was clear, and I responded. I was pregnant within a month.

Abigail Jo was born when her big sister, Elinor, was almost six years old. Every day she lives up to the meaning of her name: *God is gracious, God is joy*. Our sweet son, David, followed her two short years later. Holding him in our arms and looking into his bright eyes is a miracle to each member of our small family.

Passing through this time of doubt and fear, I grew in my relationship with my Heavenly Father and in my ability to trust Him—but not because of Abigail's and David's births. My answer had come quietly, peacefully, in the temple years before. Long before we received the blessing we were seeking, Heavenly Father filled me with His love. And I know He will guide me and bless me as I follow His plan for me. I don't know what the future holds for our small family. But I know that God knows. And where He leads me, I will follow.

Stronger
I didn't ask God to let go of my hand
So I could learn what it means to stand alone
And come back to hold His hand again.
I didn't ask God to send me through the fires of grief
To be tempered and purified
So I could emerge stronger.
I didn't ask for humility
At the cost of falling to the bottom
And viewing my small, simple life
Through insignificant eyes.
I didn't ask to have my heart's desire
Wrenched from my outstretched hands
To teach me dependence, faith, and unselfishness.
I didn't want to walk in darkness
Even for a few hours
To learn that there is One who knows the way,
One who sees the light,
Even when I cannot;
That I can trust in that One
Always.

I didn't ask for these things,
But my God, who loves me, gave them to me anyway
So I could grow stronger,
And He cried with me
While I grew.

Heather Clark, who lives in Orem, Utah, is a writer of young adult and children's fiction. She is a mother to two darling daughters and one sweet son, and a wife to one fabulous husband who shares her passion for writing and takes her hiking in beautiful places all over Utah. Heather is also a professional photographer and a former high school French teacher.

And they went forth whithersoever they were led
by the Spirit of the Lord.

—Alma 21:16

What Would I Say?

By Sally Swanson

In connection with my calling as Relief Society president, I had a very strong feeling one day to visit a particular family. I immediately got in the car to go. But as I drove to the bottom of the hill where they lived, a different spirit came over me—a spirit of doubt. In my mind, questions arose. *What am I doing? I just visited them last week. What am I going to say? I can't think of a reason to stop by. I will feel stupid.*

So I just drove past the house. Then the battle with myself began, and I decided to turn back. Two times I turned around. It was ridiculous! Finally, I thought, *This is my calling. I am entitled to inspiration for those of my stewardship. I don't know what I'll say to this sister, but I'm going to the door!*

I parked in front of their house, got out, walked to the door, and rang the bell. Her husband came to the door and greeted me from his wheelchair, relieved to see me. He had been in a motorcycle accident sometime earlier and was limited in what he could do.

Before I could say anything, he said, "I am so glad you are here! Come in! My wife is really sick, and I don't know what to do. I've called the doctor, and she needs medicine, but I can't go."

I went into the house and found my friend lying on the couch, burning up with fever. I stroked her head, and a strong feeling of love for this couple poured over me. "Yes, of course I will get her medicine."

I went to the store and picked up the medication. When I returned, I shared with them my experience of receiving the prompting that I should visit, but I didn't have any idea why. Then the husband explained to me that he had been praying fervently for someone to come . . . and then he'd heard the doorbell ring and found me standing on his doorstep! That greatly touched my heart.

Of course, I didn't tell him of the battle I'd had getting there. It was a great lesson about listening to the Spirit, and one I've never forgotten. I know the Lord watches over all of us, and he can bring help to our door . . . or send us to help others when we listen and respond to the Spirit.

Sally Swanson is a mother of six children—two redheads, two blondes, and two brunettes. Variety is the spice of life, she says. Her children, all married, have given her sixteen grandchildren. Her favorite things to do always involve family. They love playing games, camping, swimming, gathering for Sunday dinners, and just being together. She and her husband reside in South Jordan, Utah.

Learn of me, and listen to my words; walk in the meekness of my Spirit, and you shall have peace in me.
—*D&C 19:23*

Learning to Recognize the Spirit

By Bill Willson

In the fall of 1972, because of a downturn in the construction industry in California, I changed my job classification from construction surveyor to carpenter and took a more permanent job with a large power company. Our crew was building foundations for substations, and we moved around a lot. This meant leaving my wife and three daughters at times for long periods.

I missed having family with me, especially since my mother had recently passed away, and I knew of few other relatives. My father and mother separated when I was five, and we learned of my father's death when I was eleven. As far as I knew, my only living relatives were my two half-sisters and my dad's older brother and his wife, who lived near us in the San Francisco Bay area.

In addition to having few relatives, I was the only member of the Church in my immediate family. In 1953, I was baptized as a teenager and was converted mainly to the basketball and Saturday-night dance part of the Church. I became truly converted and active a year before getting married in 1962. For many reasons, starting my own family meant a great deal to me.

By the summer of 1975, I was in Eureka working at Humboldt Bay Power Plant. It was a huge job, and we were going to be there for an extended period. I slept in my van at nearby campgrounds, and I was a bit depressed, wondering why I was three hundred miles away from my family and what the Lord wanted me to do while there. The Lord tried to tell me, but I didn't listen.

As winter approached, I decided camping out at night was no longer an option, so I looked for a room to rent. Someone gave me the name of a woman, Mrs. Zacardi, who rented out rooms. As I was looking her up in the telephone directory, I browsed through the Ws for *Willson*. I had a habit of doing this because of the unusual spelling of my last name. I noticed a V. H. H. Willson and did a double take. Yes, there really were two *Ls* in Willson, just the same way I spelled my name. *I wonder how we're related?* The thought passed, and I continued my search for the landlady.

After I made my call, I had a persistent thought to call this Mr. Willson, but I worried that he'd think I was crazy. As a convert, I had only limited experience with receiving promptings from the Holy Ghost. Even though I thought several more times about contacting V. H. H. Willson, I couldn't get up the nerve to call a complete stranger and ask him if we were related.

In February 1976, I was seriously injured, and after a short stay in the hospital, I was flown home in a small medical transport plane. Thoughts of Mr. Willson and the possibility of a genealogical connection faded, and I focused on rehabilitation. I changed job classifications once more because of my debilitating injury, and I went back to work in an office job. I no longer had to travel.

Several years later, Uncle Morley, my dad's older brother, passed away. We went to visit his widow, Aunt Julie. She asked me if I had ever contacted my uncle Harold.

"Who is he?" I asked.

"He's your dad's younger brother."

"I've never heard of him."

She gave me his phone number. I called him and found out he was the very same V. H. H. Willson that I had seen in the phone book while I was in Eureka. He was so glad to hear from me that when we ended the call, he was crying. My wife, children, and I visited him several times over the next few years, and he came to visit us once before he died. We were happy that our kids were blessed to have contact with a grandfather figure on my side of the family.

Because of this reconnection, I not only had the opportunity, as an adult, to see a glimpse of what my father would have been like if he had lived longer, but I also found that Uncle Harold was of similar build and appearance to my dad. I also received memorabilia that belonged to my father, which Uncle Harold had owned. This included photos of my father and the Willson clan clear back to my great-grandfather, as well as an old miniature family Bible with an inscription from my dad's grandmother to my dad's father (November 1891) and then an inscription from my dad's father and mother to my father on April 19, 1917, as my then seventeen-year-old father left to fight in WWI. This Bible became the most precious gift from my father to me by way of my uncle.

One other piece of memorabilia that I treasure is a small, ten-inch-diameter wooden ship's wheel with a photo of my father's last ship, the USCGC *Northland*. Dad sailed on this three-mast ship to Alaska during the thirties to take in mail and supplies and to bring out mail and passengers.

These cherished pieces from my past came to my attention through a kind and loving Heavenly Father, who gave me a second chance. In time, I became better at recognizing promptings and following the Spirit, which takes some practice. Now I have learned to respond quickly and to not ignore these promptings, even if I don't understand the reasoning. If I had been in tune with the Spirit back then, I could have met my uncle sooner. But the Lord, as always, was kind in prompting my aunt to ask me the question so I could come to know this wonderful uncle. I am also grateful that through meeting him, I gathered much-needed family history information, which helped me to do temple work for my progenitors.

Bill Willson lives with his wife, Marjorie, in Logan, Utah. They have three Shih Tzu, four children, three sons-in-law, seventeen grandchildren, three grandsons-in-law, and four great-grandchildren. After Bill and Marjorie both retired, they served a two-year proselyting mission in Mexico. Bill has a degree in English from Utah State University, which he earned at age sixty-five, after his retirement.

As often as thou hast inquired thou hast received instruction of my Spirit.

—*D&C 6:14*

Should I Go?

By Judy C. Olsen

My daughter Gina, a mother of four and a school teacher, had an opportunity open up for her to take students on a trip to Europe for ten days. As plans unfolded, she realized she would also be able to take along several adult chaperones to help out. She invited her sisters . . . and me.

I had never been to Europe, and the thought was quite exciting. This would be a wonderful mother-daughter time together.

As it seemed to be quite an important decision, I decided to pray to know if this was right. I was fairly confident about the outcome of my prayer, so when I felt I should *not* go, I was surprised. Really? I shouldn't go? No one else apparently felt that way. In fact, the others were very excited. No one seemed the least anxious or felt any qualms whatsoever.

So why shouldn't *I* go? Had I really received an answer to prayer? My daughters encouraged me to come along, and I couldn't see why not. Yet I'd had enough experience in listening to the Spirit to know I had better pay attention. So in the end, I said no to my first possible trip to Europe.

For several months, preparations filled the air, and everyone had fun calling each other and making plans and going over itineraries. At last, the day came that they were to board a plane in Salt Lake City and leave. And I was left behind. I could see no real reason for it, and part of me wanted to just jump on that plane with my daughters and daughter-in-law! I wandered around the house, feeling kind of depressed and even a little stupid about my decision to stay home.

That same week, we received news that my husband's brother, Robert, had had a death in his family. His mother-in-law had passed away. The funeral would be held six hours away in Las Vegas. We didn't know her, so we had no plans to attend the funeral, which was to be held in three days. So as sad as that was, it wasn't a real reason for me to have stayed behind. Was this one of those times when I would never know why?

Three days later, we got a phone call at midnight from Robert's wife. She and Robert had been visiting with the extended family after her mother's funeral. Robert said he didn't feel well and left to go home. He went inside and apparently had a heart attack and died before help came. He was only forty-two years old.

His wife left the funeral of her mother to go to the side of her husband. It was a staggering blow to her and to their two girls.

Robert was the youngest of four children. He was much beloved by everyone. His death due to heart failure took us all by surprise. After receiving the news in the middle of the night, my husband, Don, sat in the darkened family room and grieved. We left for Las Vegas in the morning, where we went through all of the various duties that had to be performed in connection with Robert's passing.

How grateful I was that I had listened to a prompting that had come many months before to *stay home*. My husband needed me by his side that week. I realized how kind and merciful the Lord had been to *both* of us on that occasion.

Judy C. Olsen and her husband, Donald, are the parents of four married children and have sixteen grandchildren. They live in Sandy, Utah, where Judy continues to write books for Covenant, enjoy her work in various Church callings, and improve her talents in drawing.

Let all bitterness, and wrath, and anger, and clamour, and evil speaking,
be put away from you, with all malice: And be ye kind one to another,
tenderhearted, forgiving one another, even as God
for Christ's sake hath forgiven you.

—Ephesians 4:31–32

Belated Reunion

By Carolyn Campbell

Late one night, my husband and I received a telephone call to inform us that his stepmother, Mary, had passed away. Hearing the news brought immediate memories of the only three times I had seen her . . . fifteen years before. She had been drinking and seemed coarse, gruff, and unfriendly. I knew my husband and his brothers felt that their parents' marriage had failed because of this woman. My husband told me that the one time when he'd phoned to talk to his father, Mary had answered. When she'd realized he was one of her husband's children, she'd shouted, "What do *you* want?"

At first, I disagreed when my husband did not want to invite her to our wedding. Yet after I met her in person, I'm ashamed to admit that I felt she would not be a positive influence around either us or our future children. After three visits, our acquaintance dwindled to just Christmas cards with only our names signed. Then we completely lost contact with both my father-in-law and his wife. Over the years, the Spirit would touch my heart occasionally, and I would think of them. I would contemplate with sadness how quickly our relationship had completely unraveled. Sometimes I would consider reaching out to them. I would nearly summon the courage—then my good intentions would get lost in the rush of everyday tasks. And I also feared awkwardness and rejection.

When the call came that Mary had died, my husband, Griff, and I were surprised to feel that we should take our children to her funeral to see his father, who was still living. It seemed like an unexpected prompting of the Spirit, urging us past our previous reluctant feelings. It was a little scary, and we didn't know what to expect, but we moved ahead. At the viewing, we were surprised to see that Mary's funeral was being held in a Relief Society room rather than a mortuary and that ward members would speak at her services.

Her Relief Society president told us that Mary had stopped drinking five years earlier and had attended church often. She frequently volunteered to drive the missionaries, who called her *Grandma*. She described Mary as "truly angelic" at the time she died.

When I commented that Mary's face looked beautiful and kind as she lay in her casket, her friend responded that over the years, Mary's countenance had softened as her spirit had become increasingly gentle and she grew closer to God. The friend said that a week before Mary died, there was a radiance and white light about her face. At the funeral, I met my husband's cousins for the first time. One friendly, outgoing woman was within one year of my age. I knew that most of his family lived in Pennsylvania, far from Utah where we lived. While I knew that his father's three brothers had moved to Utah to work at Geneva Steel, a large company outside of Orem, the thought that my husband might have cousins in the area had never occurred to me before. He hadn't invited them to our wedding and had never mentioned them to me.

For the first time, I realized how much our family had lost when we'd allowed ourselves to become estranged because of someone who seemed different and unfriendly. Not only did we lose the association with his father and his wife, but we also had no contact with his cousins from that side of the family. I realized how costly my judgments had been. How had I decided so quickly that Mary and my children would not benefit from associating with each other?

The day we went to Mary's funeral, we also stopped at the nursing home so our four children could see their grandfather. As our children eagerly gathered around the bed, I realized that they longed for this association so long denied them. Though he could hardly speak, Grandpa smiled at each child and said how good-looking and special each one was. Although they didn't know him, there was no hesitation as each child bent near the bed and shared a special moment with Grandpa.

I'm happy, and admittedly surprised, to say that the funeral marked the beginning of a change in my husband's family. A year later, they had their first-ever family reunion. While the children immediately jumped in and started playing together like they might at any typical gathering, for the adults, this marked a momentous—and sometimes tearful—occasion. Many relatives met for the first time, and some renewed an acquaintance after a decade or more without contact. The reunion spanned three days and included family games, dinners, and time to talk and get to know each other. A second reunion followed two years later.

We are now Facebook friends and often chat online. This year, a distant relative came to Utah from Pennsylvania, sparking another weeklong get-together. We visited Temple Square, went to Lagoon, and toured City Creek Center together. We are planning our third family reunion next year.

Perhaps because we went so long without it, we now cherish our togetherness and are grateful for the tugging of the Spirit that brought it about. What blessings we have enjoyed because we have put aside our misgivings and responded to the tender, righteous desires that filled our hearts at Mary's funeral. And although we never knew Mary well and missed out on her later transformation, we are grateful that, in her own way, she opened this door to unite a family once torn apart.

Carolyn Campbell is the author of three nationally published books and eight hundred magazine articles. She is also the mother of four children and has two grandchildren. Carolyn's favorite activities are reading, writing, swimming, and speaking.

For their salvation is necessary and essential to our salvation, as Paul says concerning the fathers—that they without us cannot be made perfect— neither can we without our dead be made perfect.

—D&C 128:15.

Helping Roger Bacon

By Barbara J. Morley

On January 21, 1992, I arrived at work at the Church Office Building in downtown Salt Lake City around 6:35 a.m., and a short time later I was approached by one of the sister missionaries, Sister Jenkins, who served in indexing. She asked me if I could help her clear a name through the computer program TempleReady for a friend. TempleReady held all of the temple ordinances ever done and also served as a clearinghouse for new names to be prepared to take to the temple.

Sister Jenkins handed me a family group sheet containing only three names: Henry Bacon, the father; Margaret, the mother; and their son, Roger Bacon. Roger's birth year was 1214. *1214?* I kindly explained to the sister that the work for these people had likely been done. The Family History Library had a special section called the Medieval Department, and they would have taken care of any known names before AD 1500.

Knowing this, I realized it would be a waste of my time to research these particular names. Sister Jenkins then told me how she'd come by the names.

Her son-in-law, Craig Rasmussen, had been out of work for nearly a year, she explained. He'd decided to research the possibility of learning how to smoke out bees and open a business that would bring him some income and help beekeepers.

A few weeks earlier, on January 12, he had awakened around 2:30 a.m., and since he couldn't go back to sleep, he decided to do some research on what he could burn to create a great deal of smoke. After about an hour, the thought came to him: *Old-fashioned gunpowder smokes.*

Curious, Craig looked up *gunpowder* and came across the name of the inventor: Roger Bacon. As his eye fell on the name, he suddenly became aware of the presence of someone leaning over his shoulder, looking at the page he was reading. Quietly, but clearly, he heard the person whisper, *Will you do my temple work for me?*

Heart pounding, Craig agreed.

Then he returned to researching bee smokers and eventually went back to bed. He became aware that someone—Roger—was still nearby. *You didn't even write anything down. I invented part of that which will help you in your new business. Would you please help me?* Craig got up, found a napkin, and wrote down what he remembered Roger telling him. Suddenly, he was curious. He pulled out an encyclopedia. If Roger Bacon had invented gunpowder, Craig should find a listing for him.

As Craig flipped through the pages, he could feel the keen interest of the man who seemed to be looking over his shoulder and reading along with him. Then he found it: Roger Bacon, 1214–1294, had been born in England. A great scholar in his time, he had studied Greek, Hebrew, and Latin; had investigated lenses and mirrors; and had diagramed the optic nervous system. Roger Bacon had also taught at Oxford University and then had joined the Franciscan Order and become a friar. He wrote *Compendium of Theological Studies* and *Opus Magus* (Great Knowledge). His unconventional ideas landed him in prison for many years. He was released, and then he died at Oxford in 1294.

As Craig closed the encyclopedia, stunned, he heard again the whisper of this great man. *Will you do my temple work for me?*

Yes. Of course, he agreed.

By now it was 5:30 a.m., and Craig returned to bed. Yet he felt the presence of this fine scholar still nearby. As he pulled the covers up, he heard quite loudly, *What about my family?*

This time Craig jumped out of bed, went back to the books, and began making notes of all known dates for Roger Bacon and his parents.

After Sister Jenkins had told me this, I explained to her that, even so, the work would have probably been done by now because Roger Bacon had been a well-known historical figure.

She looked at me. "Then why would this Roger come to Craig and ask him to do his temple work?"

I agreed to take the time to do the necessary research, and I finally promised her that I'd let her know the next day.

All day long, I kept putting it off. I had a heavy workload, and that day, I had nearly two hundred names to process. Yet I also noticed that all day long, the family group sheet of the Bacon family kept getting in the way on my desk. I'd set it aside, then I'd see it once more on the top of my stack of work. Finally, late in the day, I came across the Bacon family group sheet yet again, and I thought, *Okay, okay, I'll do it first thing in the morning, but it won't clear.*

I usually didn't think about work once I was home. As a busy single mom, I had too many other things to do and think about. But that night, I couldn't get the Bacon family out of my thoughts.

The next morning, I decided to leave for work a little early. I arrived at work at 6:25 a.m., and I was the only person on the floor for the next half hour. In the quiet stillness of the vast Family History Library, I checked the pre-1500s file for people whose temple work had been done.

As I did so, I could feel the presence of three people looking over my right shoulder, telling me that I wouldn't find anything because they were not there. My skepticism vanished.

I began to check all of the resources within the library system. I typed the name into TempleReady. I couldn't type fast enough. I sensed I was not alone in my cubicle. I not only felt their presence but also felt their great excitement. I hit the keys to begin the clearing process to see if the work had already been done. All three names *cleared*. Their work had not yet been done! I felt their excitement, and I could hardly contain my own emotions.

Sister Jenkins arrived around 7:00 a.m. I gave her the TempleReady disk and a printout of the names, showing they were cleared. Craig was now authorized to proceed with the sacred work on the Bacon family's behalf.

I talked with Sister Jenkins a couple of weeks later. I shared with her the experience I had had while I was checking their names before I cleared them for their work to be done. She told me the work had been completed and mentioned the date, February 1, 1992. Craig's children had had a wonderful experience doing the baptisms, as did the adults, who did the other ordinances for the Bacon family.

When she shared this joy with me, something about the date struck a chord. I went home and opened my journal to see why.

That Saturday, February 1, 1992, I had not planned to attend the temple, despite the fact that I had been attending weekly to do some endowments for my own family. I'd had a busy day planned, but as I awoke that morning, I had a strong feeling that I needed to go to the temple. As I planned to drop off my daughter at the University of Utah, I thought I would go to the Salt Lake Temple, do a quick session, then pick her up again. However, I felt impressed to drive out to the Jordan River Temple, a twenty-five-minute drive south.

When I arrived, the session I had hoped to attend had filled, and I had to wait. As I waited, I again had a strong feeling to wait for not one but two more sessions. As sessions began every twenty minutes, it wasn't a long wait, and I finally attended the 10:40 a.m. session.

During the forty-minute wait in the chapel, I sensed a strong spirit in the room, and my emotions overcame me. I had to constantly fight back tears. As the session began, my emotions deepened, if possible, and I felt the Spirit strong and sweet throughout the session. As I came through the veil into the celestial room, I heard in my mind someone say, *There she is.* I felt a sweet spirit come over me and someone greet me, hug me, and thank me. I assumed it had probably been the name of the woman whose work I had done.

As I talked with Sister Jenkins, I suddenly realized that Craig and others had been *in that session* doing the temple work for the Bacon family! The Lord had kindly guided me to be present in the temple at the same time. And I had been privileged to feel their gratitude that day.

I can testify that those on the other side of the veil do know who we are and are grateful for the work we do for them on earth. I look forward to meeting the Bacon family someday as well as all of the others for whom I have been proxy or will yet be proxy for in this great, eternal work.

I bear witness that this is the work of the Lord, that blessings come to those we do work for in the holy temples of the Lord, and blessings do come to those who do the work. I know Jesus Christ is our Savior, and His gospel is true.

Barbara Jackman Morley is the seventh of ten children raised in Woods Cross, Utah. She worked for the LDS Church's Family History Library for several years, including giving technical support for FamilySearch for four years. She enjoys reading; doing genealogy; keeping journals, pictures, and music; and especially being with family. Barbara lives with her husband, Ray, in Orem, Utah. Between them, they have twelve children and twenty-seven grandchildren.

Note: In the years since this story took place, the Church has set out a very strict policy that members only do temple work for immediate family members or those who are direct-line ancestors.

And by the power of the Holy Ghost ye may know the truth of all things.

—Moroni 10:5

My Long Road Back

By C. Jacobsen

I grew up the oldest of three children in an active Latter-day Saint family in Orem, Utah. Everyone I knew belonged to the Church, except two family friends who were Baptists. I went to church every Sunday, mostly to see my friends. While in high school, I had to work a lot on Sundays and got out of the habit of going to church. I took seminary but often skipped classes because my friends and I thought our teacher was so old and boring.

I met a young man from Provo, Utah, and we started dating. His family was not active in the Church, but he had been baptized. We married, and my husband got his first big job working for IBM in San Jose, California. His work associates, none of whom were members of the Church, became our friends. We looked forward to all of the parties and fun times we had together. Before I knew it, I was smoking and drinking whenever I was with them.

When we went back to Utah to visit our families, we always stayed with my in-laws because they were party people too. I didn't want my parents to smell smoke on me, and if they did, I could blame it on my in-laws. My sister came down to visit with us. She had a strong testimony of the Church, and when she found out my secrets, she was devastated. I made her promise not to tell Mom and Dad.

My husband and I started our family and continued our way of life. We moved several times, and I could not figure out how the Church always knew where we were. Oftentimes, a home teacher would show up, or we'd get cards in the mail, or a visiting teacher would drop by. I later learned that my sister's husband had been sending our address to Church headquarters. In some of our wards, he had even called to talk to the Relief Society president or bishop. In one ward, various people picked up my little girl and took her to Primary and Sunday School. When we visited Utah, I wanted to have my brother baptize her, but I forgot to get the papers signed by my bishop before we left, something I've always regretted.

My husband and daughter were always on my case to quit smoking. I tried to quit many times but would end up sneaking cigarettes on the side. I spent a fortune on nicotine patches and nicotine gum. I finally did quit, but I was always tempted whenever a friend smoked around me.

After we retired, we bought a home out in the country. We kept in touch with some of our old friends, but we were a long distance from them and seldom saw them. We lived in the San Joaquin valley, and our nearest neighbors were Hispanic, but we didn't speak Spanish. I was lonesome and missed being around people.

We began to receive a monthly newsletter from the Church in the mail, but the meetinghouse was an hour away. My sister encouraged me to go to Relief Society and meet some sisters who, she assured me, would become my friends. I knew my husband wouldn't go to church with me, and I wasn't brave enough to go by myself.

Then my husband had a horrible accident on his tractor and nearly lost his life waiting for help to arrive from so far away. After his recovery, we decided that at our age, we needed to be closer to a city, so we started looking for a new home. We moved to our present home in Northern California. I told my husband that we should start going to church, but week after week went by, and neither of us made any effort to go.

One Sunday afternoon, there was a knock on my door, and I opened it to see a woman and her teenage son. Linda said they were members of the Church and she was my visiting teacher. She asked if they could visit for a while. I was so lonesome that I invited them in. They stayed for a long time, and we shared a lot about what was going on in our lives.

Linda was so open, friendly, and outgoing that we talked most of the afternoon. She said that she taught the Gospel Essentials class and would love to pick me up the following Sunday if I wanted to come. I agreed.

The following Sunday, she picked me up, and there was another woman in the car, Sondra, who was investigating the Church. When I walked into the meetinghouse, familiar sights and sounds greeted me, and suddenly I felt at home. As the meeting progressed, I felt the Spirit fill me completely, and I knew this was where I wanted to be. When I went to Relief Society, the president apologized over and over for not contacting me sooner. I assured her it was all right because I probably would not have been responsive before now.

Now I wanted to learn everything that I had ignored as a youth. Week after week, Linda was faithful about picking up Sondra and me. After church, I would come home and read the Sunday School lesson for the coming week and try to be prepared for the discussion. Linda presented many gospel principles to me, and I sometimes wondered if I knew *anything* about the Church. I felt the Spirit confirming the truth to me, and this became a source of wonderment and thanksgiving. I realized the Lord knew me and loved me, and that became an overpowering testimony that sustained me throughout my journey back into activity.

During this time, my sister often called me, and we had many long talks about the gospel. I asked her many questions. At last we had something in common to talk about, and after so many years, we were finally building a close relationship. She answered many questions that I thought were too embarrassing or too simple to ask in class.

I loved having new friends, and soon the bishop called me to my first Church calling, working with the Primary activity-day girls. It was then that I met Hazel, and we have been best friends ever since. Four months after I started back, Sondra joined the Church.

During this time, I was diagnosed with breast cancer. It was scary, but I felt in my heart that it was going to be okay. Not only my sister but also ward members rallied around to support me during my recovery. Friends brought in food, sent cards, and showered me with love and friendship. Many sisters surprised me at a special luncheon on my final day of radiation, and we all celebrated together. Presently, I am a cancer survivor.

One special incident during that time will forever remain with me. After my first chemo treatment, I had a terrible headache that wouldn't go away. I suffered and tossed and turned in bed. I finally got out of bed, knelt down, and asked the Lord to take the pain away. By the time I got back in bed, it was gone. I marveled that He knew me personally and had healed me.

I learned that truth and a testimony of the gospel come slowly, line upon line. The many blessings and prayers from the ward, friends, and family saved my life.

I started paying my tithing. Linda and her husband were our home teachers, and my husband came in often and listened to their messages. I was worried about whether he would accept this wonderful new perspective I had gained. He became friends with the home teachers and finally said it was okay for them to leave with a prayer.

While visiting my sister in Utah one day, we walked through Temple Square. I looked up at the temple and told her I was going to go in there someday. With tears in our eyes, we both agreed that it was going to happen.

The following year, in October, I received my endowment in the Mount Timpanogos Temple. Even though my parents were active, they did not get sealed in the temple until after I was married, so on that October day, our family joined together for the first time within temple walls. I was sealed to my parents, brother, and sister. We became an eternal family. Linda and Rob, Sondra, and Dorothy, all friends from California, flew to Utah to be with me for my special occasion. That week, my sister and I went to the Salt Lake Temple, a dream fulfilled.

My life has completely changed from just a few years ago. I hardly remember my old party life. My days are filled with going to the Fresno California Temple, fixing meals for new mothers, going to lunch with friends, preparing baskets for the elderly in our ward, helping with funerals and meals, serving in Church callings, feeding the elders, exercising with friends, giving service at the Salvation Army, taking our turn to prepare a sacrament meeting program for a small branch near Yosemite Park, picking grapes at the welfare farm, visiting teaching, being with family, and all of the other many activities that come with Church membership.

I teach my grandchildren about the gospel and try to live my life as an example to my husband and children. If it weren't for my visiting teacher, Linda, knocking on my door, none of this would have happened. I love my new life now. My husband's heart has softened, and he has participated in activities with me and has listened to home teachers. He gives service to my widow friends and supports me in my callings. I hope that one day my husband, daughters, and granddaughters will want to experience the joy that I have found in the gospel.

Sister Jacobsen lives in Northern California with her husband. They are the parents of two girls and have two granddaughters. They love to garden and to work in their yard filled with fruit trees. Harvesting fruit and home canning are a special joy. She and her husband like to travel and go camping, fishing, and jet skiing with their family. Sister Jacobsen walks, swims, loves garage sales, goes to lunch, and attends the temple with her new friends. She enjoys cooking and, as the compassionate service leader, takes many meals into ward members' homes.

He Knows Our Hearts' Desires

And we know that all things work together for good to them that love God.

—Romans 8:28

Faith and Works

By Ingrid Brockbank

From the day I was born in the middle of war-ravaged Berlin in 1943, the hand of the Lord has been evident in my life. When I was an infant, my mother hid with me in the basement of an apartment building for ten days, with only one potato a day for us to share, as the Russians invaded the city. Through bombings, invasions, and severe deprivations, my life was spared. Later on, my father was inspired to leave East Berlin before the wall went up. Although we lived as refugees starting over with nothing, the Lord was guiding me to the time and place where I would be taught the gospel and be introduced to the worthy man who would become my husband. After I was baptized, I came to America and spent the next four decades raising a family and facing both the joys and sorrows that life brings us all.

One of my deepest sorrows was losing my husband to cancer at the young age of fifty-four. Like so many times before, I found myself starting over, making a new life one day at a time. Without the peace of the gospel, my life would have been bleak. Instead, I found strength to continue and many happy experiences to share with my family as it grew grandchild by grandchild.

In May 2010, I traveled to Germany with some of my children and grandchildren to visit relatives. It was a gift to be able to strengthen family bonds and see the beauties of the land of my birth through my grandchildren's eyes. I was deeply grateful to the Lord for this blessing, and I enjoyed every minute of our trip.

But within only a few days of returning home to Utah, I found myself unable to regain my energy. At first, I didn't think too much about it. Even my daughters had some jet lag, so it wasn't unusual that, being older, it would take me a little longer to get readjusted.

Through June and July, my fatigue persisted. I was invited to spend a weekend at Lake Powell with some of my family, and I gladly accepted. Maybe all I needed was some sunshine and relaxation to get my pep back. But when I returned home, I realized something deeper was wrong. The golden glow that I thought was the beginnings of a nice tan had spread to my eyes. I knew enough to realize I had jaundice, and I immediately scheduled a doctor's appointment. My doctor was concerned as well, and before long, I was receiving the news no one wants to hear: it was cancer—pancreatic cancer, specifically.

Average life expectancy for pancreatic cancer patients is generally less than six months after a diagnosis, making it one of the deadliest cancers. My first thought was, "I'm not ready to leave my family yet." My husband had died when our oldest grandchild was not even two. I felt strongly that they still needed their grandmother. Although I felt deep concern for my family, I personally felt very calm, as if I were wrapped in the Lord's arms, comforted and sheltered. I thought of 2 Timothy 1:7: "For God hath not given us the spirit of fear; but of power, and of love, and of a sound mind."

After I returned home, I knelt in prayer and humbly pleaded with my Heavenly Father that if it be His will, I might be healed from this cancer for my family's sake. I was willing to accept His will in my life, but after praying, I received the strong impression that, in addition to submitting to the Lord's decision, I should also do whatever was within my abilities to help in the healing process.

There's an old Russian proverb that I have often applied in my life: If your boat is sinking, pray to God, but row for the shore. Faith requires submission to our Heavenly Father's wisdom, but it also requires righteous action. In Elder Cornish's October 2011 conference talk, he reminds us that "it is contrary to the economy of heaven for the Lord to do for us that which we can do for ourselves." Although I knew that only with God's grace and power was there any chance for a miracle, I felt plain as day that my Father in Heaven wanted me to be an active participant in this experience.

I started reading and researching everything I could find about cancer. Rather than getting discouraged about the poor prognosis of this disease, I trusted that the Lord would guide me in my efforts to get well. My life was a whirlwind of changes as I learned to juice, started an exercise regimen, cut out all sugar, and began an ultrahealthy diet. Through it all, I knew the Lord was watching over me and guiding my path. This was confirmed to me time and again through many miracles, small and large.

I came to see blessings even in frustrating, painful events. Once, because the cancer was blocking my bile duct, the doctors operated and put in a stent. Within a few days, it became infected. They decided to send me to a specialist at Huntsman Cancer Center. This time, the operation was a success. But more importantly, the surgeon asked if my case had been reviewed by anyone at Huntsman and offered to schedule an appointment. My painful infection actually led me to the oncological team that treated me with skill and kindness.

Another miracle was that, initially, it was thought that I would not be a candidate for surgery because it appeared that the cancer may have spread to my liver. As I continued to pray, I felt strongly that I would be a good prospect for the surgery. A second PET scan showed my liver to be clear after all, and I underwent the complicated Whipple surgery that removed part of my pancreas, upper intestine, and gallbladder. Although recovery time for this surgery can range upwards of two weeks in the hospital, I was walking the day after the surgery and went home after only six days. The wonderful surgeon who performed the procedure was one of the most skilled in the world, more evidence that I was continually guided to those in a position to best help me.

Every day is a precious gift, and I am inexpressibly grateful for the extra time I have been granted. I am so touched by the countless ways my Heavenly Father has blessed me through this trial. I was blessed to be guided to the best hospital and doctors available. I was blessed with courage and good cheer throughout my ordeal. I was blessed by a great number of people who kept me in their prayers—from my cousins in Germany who lit candles at mass to the friends who kept my name on the temple prayer roll to the ward members who held many fasts to the wonderful priesthood leaders who gave blessings that sustained and comforted me.

I am humbled when I think of how many people of deep faith ask Heavenly Father to be spared for another season, only to be told with great love that now is their time to come home, like my dear companion. I am mindful every day that I bear a sacred responsibility to use this precious gift of time wisely. I bear witness that God is with us at all times and that He truly does consecrate all our experiences for our good, even if our mortal vision makes it difficult at times to see.

Ingrid Brockbank is a mother of four and grandmother of eleven. She lives in Alpine, Utah. Ingrid is an avid reader and loves traveling. In her spare time, she makes handmade appliqué quilts.

A new heart also will I give you, and a new spirit will I put within you: and I will take away the stony heart out of your flesh, and I will give you an heart of flesh.

—*Ezekiel 36:26*

Could I Sustain Him?

By Katherine Newheart

On one memorable Sunday, ward members were advised that there would be a change in the bishopric the following week. The usual rumor mill began to buzz, and I, along with some close friends, speculated who might be called as the new bishop. We chatted that we'd be fine with just about any brother in the ward—except one: Brother Michaels (not his real name).

Due to several small problems in the past, I had finally concluded that he was young and inexperienced, quick to judge, lacked humility, and besides that, he had a young family that needed him.

He lived in the house behind us, separated only by our backyard and a chain-link fence, so I could see clearly into his yard, and he could see into ours. Once, when he had served as elders quorum president, he'd quipped that people often put their best effort into their front yards, but you should see their backyards. Was this directed at us or just a passing remark? We'd approached him about putting in a solid fence, but he'd disagreed about which kind to install and refused to compromise, even when we volunteered to pay more than half the cost. We let it go. Yet we felt uncomfortable entertaining in our backyard, which was so open to our neighbors.

When Brother Michaels dug a large hole for an inground trampoline close to the fence, he severed the root system of a lovely tree in our yard, nearly killing it. And when ward members rallied around to build him an extension to his home, his children threw discarded building supplies over the fence into our yard. And so it went. My irritation with him grew every year, and I finally avoided going into my yard at all. As a result, I felt more and more like a prisoner in my own home.

So that day, as my friends and I talked about who might be called, a number of us shared our grievances concerning Brother Michaels. We agreed we didn't like him because we didn't feel that humility was his strong suit, and for us, that seemed reason enough not to call him to such an important position. However, because Brother Michaels had been called to the stake high council a couple of years earlier, he was an obvious person to interview.

I recalled that at the time of his call to the high council, my concern had been so great that I had taken it to the Lord in prayer. Because this brother had repeatedly hurt my feelings, I expressed my concerns to my Father in Heaven that his being on the high council might potentially put him in a position one day to receive a calling as bishop. I received a sweet reassurance that things would be just fine, which I interpreted as he would never be called to serve as a bishop—at least not in our ward.

The next Sunday when the stake president presented Brother Michaels's name to the congregation for a sustaining vote as the new bishop, I almost let out an audible gasp. One of my dear friends left the meeting in tears. Another went home after sacrament meeting. I went home during Sunday School, feeling hurt and betrayed. How could the Lord have given me that feeling of peace two years earlier?

When I returned for Relief Society, another friend turned to me and asked where I had been during Sunday School. I told her I'd needed to take a breather. She too expressed her concerns and told me I wasn't the only one.

After church, my sweet husband and I went for a long walk. We talked about why I was feeling the way I did. He shared his concerns with me as well. I will never forget what he said: "You need to understand just how great your influence is among the sisters in the ward. Satan will try to use you to undermine the confidence of the ward members in this new bishop. You need to accept this as the Lord's will."

I knew he was right, but I still felt hurt, my confidence shaken.

The next day I told my kids to give me a little space. I went into my room, closed the door, and poured my heart out to my Heavenly Father in a way I hadn't for years. I expressed my desire to follow His will. I pleaded for understanding and peace.

Then I decided to go for a walk—a very long walk. I had no destination or purpose except to continue to ponder and pray. As I walked, the words to the very last verse of "How Firm a Foundation" (*Hymns*, no. 85) would not leave my head:

> The soul that on Jesus hath leaned for repose
> I will not, I cannot, desert to his foes;
> That soul, though all hell should endeavor to shake,

I'll never, no never, I'll never, no never,
I'll never, no never, no never forsake!

Was I the soul that hell was endeavoring to shake? And was the Lord telling me he'd never, ever forsake me? I tried to get the words out by singing other hymns, but that hymn just kept coming back, especially the fourth and fifth verses:

When through the deep waters I call thee to go,
The rivers of sorrow shall not thee o'erflow,
For I will be with thee, thy troubles to bless,
And sanctify to thee, And sanctify to thee,
And sanctify to thee thy deepest distress.

When through fiery trials thy pathway shall lie,
My grace, all sufficient, shall be thy supply.
The flame shall not hurt thee; I only design
Thy dross to consume, Thy dross to consume,
Thy dross to consume and thy gold to refine.

My Heavenly Father knew I was under siege by adversarial forces trying to shake me. He knew that not only was I in distress, but I was also in need of refining. I realized there was a reason for that hymn, so as I headed back home, I embraced it and sang all of the verses. As difficult as this was, the Lord would not forsake me as I tried to understand and accept His will.

When I knelt in prayer that night, I thanked Heavenly Father for insight and for His love and confidence in my ability to overcome this trial. But I still wasn't wholly past it yet.

The next day I awoke with a feeling of peace, but as the day wore on, my anxiety returned. I spoke to one of my best friends about what I was feeling. She suggested that we both just buy new houses and move from the ward! As tempting as that was, I knew in my heart that it wasn't the answer. By the day's end, my feelings of hurt and betrayal were back.

This pattern continued. Each morning for the rest of the week, when I awoke, my heart was at peace, but as the day wore on, the injustices welled up. Bit by bit, throughout each successive day, my heart was softened a little more, and slowly, love began to fill a place where only hurt, irritation, and anger had been. By the following Sunday morning, my heart had given way completely. I looked forward to shaking the new bishop's hand and smiling at him.

Still, I was nervous as I entered the chapel. I looked at the new bishopric seated on the stand, and then I felt my heart fill with compassion toward Bishop Michaels. I *knew* he had been called of God. I knew the stake president had been inspired to extend such a call.

Later, as I handed him my tithing envelope, I smiled, looked him in the eye, and said, "Thank you for accepting this calling. I know you'll do just fine."

Looking back, I had become lax in studying the scriptures, attending the temple, and praying with much sincerity. And I had been drawn into talking negatively about someone else instead of keeping it in the family or with the Lord. A change began that day on many fronts.

My husband and I made the decision that from that moment on we would refrain from speaking evil of the Lord's anointed. As we ceased to criticize, our children no longer seemed irritated by this family. I took time to visit with some of the sisters with whom I had previously engaged in critical talk about this man and shared my personal experience with them. I tried to make amends for my previous actions.

A few weeks later, I had an opportunity to talk to the sister who had left the meeting in tears. I asked her how she was doing and briefly shared my experience with her. She told me that she too had received a similar witness. That made me happy to hear. I could feel the Lord watching over all of us and helping us.

The day came that I finally talked to the bishop about my feelings and shared with him the witness I had received. It was after I talked with him that I realized the feelings were clearly one-sided on my part and that neither he nor his family had harbored ill feelings toward me or my family.

This was a very difficult experience for me, and yet I learned what it felt like to have my heart softened. Hurt feelings are tender feelings, and we don't always want to give them up because it can feel like it somehow trivializes what happened. Yet healing from the Lord comes when we are willing to let Him judge the situation completely and then ask for His help in finding peace again. I am grateful that the Lord led me along, little by little, until my heart healed completely.

Katherine Newheart is a wife and mother who lives in Northern Utah. She enjoys spending time outdoors with her family. In her free time, she enjoys reading, writing, working on her scrapbooks, and running.

Remember the sabbath day, to keep it holy.

—Exodus 20:8

What Should I Do?

By Gordon Thelin

My father died when I was only eighteen months old, so my mom had to be both a mom and a dad to me. I remember that one of the best lessons my mother taught me occurred when I was eleven years old.

I was preparing for my second season of playing soccer, and I started practicing with the team midsummer. At the end of August, the game schedule came out. All of the games were to be played on Sunday mornings. I couldn't believe it. My family didn't play sports on Sundays. We went to church and did quiet, spiritual activities that day.

I told my mother about the Sunday games and asked, "What should I do?"

My mom told me that since I had practiced with the team in preparation for the first game and that since the team was counting on me to be there, I should go ahead and play the first game. She then told me she would let me decide about the rest of the season.

This was to be my decision, then. I remember praying about it and trying to figure out what I should do. I wanted to play, but I also wanted to do what was right. I didn't tell my mom what I was going to do, and she didn't ask.

After the first game, I went up to the coach and explained the situation to him and told him that I didn't think I should play the rest of the season. He was nice and told me he understood. When I found my mom, she asked me what I'd talked to the coach about. I told her about my decision. She told me how proud she was and that she had known I would make the right decision.

That one act of faith on my mother's part made a huge impact on me. I decided I never wanted to disappoint her in any way. I wanted to always act in a way that would make her proud.

This experience also helped to shape my actions many years later in life when I became a father.

When my son Jeffrey was about twelve, he bought a video game with his own money. He played the first several levels and absolutely loved it. Then, a few days later, he came to me and told me that he had reached a level in the game that he wasn't sure about. He said that he felt like some of the characters were kind of evil and he felt uncomfortable.

I was impressed that Jeffrey had come to me to ask advice instead of just playing the game. I told him I would have to think about it and do some research. If I told him it would be okay to continue, he would be able to play his game with a clear conscience, perhaps ignoring his own initial misgivings. It is important to understand that Jeffrey usually had a way of pestering his mother and me until he got his way. He wanted me to make the decision. So it was no surprise to me that he kept bugging me about it and begging me to let him play that level.

Finally, I thought about what I had learned from my mother. An idea came to me that would place the decision where it belonged. I told Jeffrey that he should pray about the game, go play a level, and then pray again. I expressed my faith in him that he would make the right decision.

A little while later, Jeffrey came to me and said, "Thanks a lot, Dad! I won't be playing *that* game ever again."

And to my knowledge, he never did.

I am grateful to my mother, who taught me the importance of letting children seek and recognize their own guidance from the Lord. I could have created a rule, set a guideline, or tried in some other way to create a safe place for my son. But letting him go to the Lord himself taught him in a way much more effective than anything I could have done.

Gordon Thelin lives in Virginia with his wife, Jan, and their five children. For many years, he has been a soccer coach for his children's teams and an advocate in the community for Saturday games. Gordon also enjoys sailing, skiing, and rock climbing with his family. At church, Gordon serves as a Primary teacher for the Valiant 10 class.

And ye will not suffer your children that they go hungry, or naked; neither will ye suffer that they transgress the laws of God, and fight and quarrel one with another, and serve the devil, who is the master of sin, or who is the evil spirit which hath been spoken of by our fathers, he being an enemy to all righteousness.

—*Mosiah 4:14*

Stretched to the Breaking Point

By Mike Chadwick

In April 2009, I had been serving for only a year as the bishop of the Chugach Foothills Ward in Anchorage, Alaska. My wife, Mandy, and I were expecting our sixth child. Winter had been long and dark, as usual, and things were just starting to look up. Mandy was usually the most sick during the first three months of pregnancy, so the recent twelve-week mark of her pregnancy had been a welcomed event.

However, I was about to learn one meaning of Mosiah 4:14, which speaks of not allowing your children to go hungry or naked, in a very real and personal way.

On Thursday, April 23, 2009, I was nearing home after a day at work when I received a call on my cell phone. To conserve resources, I had purchased a phone with limited minutes. Since I was close to home, I ignored the call. The phone rang a second time as I approached the house. As I exited the car, my children darted toward me exclaiming, "Mom is bleeding!" I ran upstairs and found Mandy flush with panic and in the throes of a possible miscarriage.

I quickly made arrangements for the children and dashed to the hospital with Mandy. After waiting quite some time, the doctor performed an ultrasound. All we could see was the baby's back and no movement. After the medical team took some measurements and pictures, I asked, "Is the baby moving?"

The doctor indicated that the baby was moving, and Mandy burst into tears of relief. Unfortunately, a blood clot had formed and attached itself to the membranes that kept amniotic fluid safely cushioning the baby. Because of the bleeding, there was only a fifty-fifty chance that the baby would survive.

Soon afterward, Brother Richard Walker joined me, and we gave Mandy a priesthood blessing. They sent Mandy home with instructions to go on bed rest and take it easy until her next doctor appointment the following Tuesday.

Late that night, I pondered what the future would bring. This was certainly unexpected. What was I to do? I was working full time for the municipality of Anchorage. I was the bishop of a wonderful ward. I was the father of five children ranging from eighteen months to ten years of age.

In addition, we still had about three weeks of school left, which limited my babysitter options. I thought of several sisters who could possibly help, but many of them worked or had their own challenges. I decided to wait until Tuesday to see what the doctor had to say. Perhaps everything would "just disappear" and Mandy would be healed.

On Tuesday, we went to the doctor. Thankfully, he took Mandy off of bed rest. However, she received strict instructions to not be jarred, lift anything, cough hard, vomit, go upstairs, or allow the kids to bump into her. Now that I had better information, a plan began to form. My dad had recently retired, so I decided to fly him up to help Mandy and care for the kids until the school year ended. Once school ended, babysitters would be available to take my dad's place. In addition, I needed to step up my own efforts. I was suddenly feeding and dressing the children and doing a hundred other things that Mandy used to do.

Daily life soon fell into a rhythm. However, a few weeks later, at Mandy's next doctor appointment, we could tell the doctor was still worried. "There is a lot going on in here," he told us. We learned that the internal bleeding was worsening for several reasons and that the baby had blood in its bowels.

Although I am not a doctor, this did not sound good. Mandy was put on complete bed rest—flat on her back until the baby's due date more than four months away in October. At this time, we also found out the baby was a little girl. We had never asked the gender of our previous five children, but this time, Mandy wanted to have a better idea and feel a deeper connection with the small baby struggling to live.

I rearranged the house and moved a bed downstairs between the kitchen and the family room. This is where all the action occurred, and Mandy could help keep an eye on the children. Once again, we soon fell into a rhythm. I would get up early, prepare breakfast, set out the children's clothing, and then go to work. The children would awaken, wander downstairs, and eat breakfast with Mandy supervising the action from bed. The babysitter would arrive at 9:00 a.m. and leave at 2:00 p.m. From 2:00 p.m. until 5:00 p.m., Mandy supervised the younger children from the bed with the help of the older children.

This began a season in our lives that put intense pressure on me. Time at home could no longer be used for my own many responsibilities. Everything that had once run smoothly under Mandy's care now stared me in the face.

Mealtimes, with all they required, plus cleanup, staying ahead of the laundry, choosing clothing and dressing the little ones, playtimes and bedtimes—all took enormous amounts of time. I was getting up earlier and going to bed later. And I had very little time to study or meditate on the many responsibilities I carried outside the family. I experienced quite literally what happened if I did not provide in ways that kept my children from going hungry or naked. That scripture in Mosiah, which I had always interpreted to mean I should provide for my family, took on a very literal meaning.

After the school year ended, I attended a stake youth conference. I took Siera, my youngest child, who was only eighteen months old, with me and left the other children at home, basically to care for themselves with Mandy's limited direction.

The unrelenting pace was beginning to take a toll on me. On the Sunday after youth conference, I wasn't feeling well, but I still attended to my church duties: early morning meetings, then sacrament meeting, and other meetings scheduled for the afternoon. The stake president visited our sacrament meeting and sat next to me on the stand. He asked how things were going and then whispered to me, "Let the ward help the bishop." Quite frankly, I did not recall ever asking for any significant help from ward members in my entire life. I was usually the one providing service, not receiving it.

In early June, while at work, I received a frantic phone call from my wife. The Relief Society sisters, by way of a request from our Relief Society president, Tina Halcomb, had showed up and were cleaning the house. This came as a surprise. Mandy did not try to stop them, since she knew they would ignore her protests. But I was horrified. I had managed to keep the downstairs looking fairly neat and tidy; however, since visitors did not go upstairs, that was another story. I paced my office floor thinking, *What's upstairs? Did I ever take those dishes dirtied by late night snacks out of the bathroom sink? Is Carson's bed still covered with toys from an aborted cleaning effort? Oh, just please go home.*

As I arrived home that night, I walked into a spit-spot polished home. I had to admit that those wonderful sisters had dug me out of a pit. They saw a stubborn bishop and set him straight. In fact, it was a relief not to see things waiting to be done everywhere I looked.

From that initial cleaning effort, additional help arrived, and I felt that we could make this bed rest work. I washed the clothes late at night, put them in the dryer, and then removed them the next morning. Each week, one sister stopped by to fold laundry I dumped into the baby's portable crib, and two sisters provided dinner on Tuesdays and Wednesdays.

Early that summer, I received some unwanted, but not unexpected, news from my employer. Revenue shortfalls would require me to take unpaid leave from work. Finances were already tight with the cost of daily babysitters and additional medical procedures. However, this work furlough provided me an opportunity to be home with my wife and children every other Friday. It turned out to be a significant blessing. In addition, some extended family members donated funds to help with the babysitters, another significant blessing.

As time went on, the dark winter turned into summer. And that Alaskan summer turned out to be one of the most beautiful summers we had had since moving there in 2002. It was absolutely gorgeous, and Mandy was on bed rest! You have to understand: after going through a long, dark, cold winter, folks in Alaska play very hard in the summer, especially since we have sunlight almost twenty-four hours a day. I offered to take the kids hooligan fishing, dip netting for red salmon, and on other adventures. All I heard Mandy say was, "Mike, are you telling me that you are going to take our young children to dangerous waters without life jackets as the only adult and keep an eye on them while you fish?"

Sort of. I was going to provide life jackets. Well, I ended up foregoing many of our typical summer adventures. Once again, the blessings came. We had several friends provide us with red salmon that year, and we were able to stock our freezer as in past years.

We faced the question of attending a family reunion that we had anticipated for four years. The children really wanted to get on the big jet that would fly them to Seattle, Washington. After consulting doctors and others, Mandy was left in the care of our ward Relief Society president, and the children were given the opportunity to meet relatives and see cousins in Seattle.

Boarding the plane to Seattle with five small children turned a lot of heads and created a bit of a stir. I was prepared for this trip—or so I thought. As soon as the plane started its ascent, I gave the kids fruit snacks to keep their ears clear, and I gave my eighteen-month-old girl, Siera, a bottle. No sooner had the kids dozed off then Siera vomited the entire bottle onto my lap. The fasten-seat-belt light was still on, so I waited and then darted to the restroom at the first opportunity. I cleaned Siera off the best I could and tried to clean myself off. I ended up just using a bunch of smelly airplane soap and spreading it all over our clothes. Oh well.

While in Washington, I called Mandy several times each day. Although I felt everything would be just fine, I hated to be away from her. I was also particularly sensitive to my role as bishop and the possible perception ward members might have that I had abandoned my wife in her time of need. However, we had consulted doctors and prayed about this trip and felt everything would be okay.

Mandy continued her bed rest throughout the summer. As the due date approached, the doctor gradually let her sit up in bed. Her mother came to visit for our son Wyatt's baptism, which we had delayed since May because of the bed rest. Mandy attended the baptism using a wheelchair. It was nice to have the entire family attend a church event.

On Sunday, October 11, I attended my early-morning church meetings as usual. Then I raced home to pick up the kids for church. As usual, I had put out all their clothes the night before, and they had gotten themselves ready under Mandy's direction. As I left that morning, Mandy looked like she was starting to have contractions.

A half hour later, during the middle of sacrament meeting, my cell phone vibrated two different times, very close together. This was the sign that we had developed to let me know that Mandy needed me immediately. I asked a deacon sitting on the stand to call my wife to see what she needed. He seemed to take forever to get back to me. When he returned, he told me that Mandy said, "Come home now. The baby is on its way." I leaned over to my first counselor, told him he was now presiding, and walked off the stand.

Brooke was born later that evening. Everything went fine, and thankfully the baby seemed normal. That evening, we took a picture of me holding Brooke in my arms as she looked up and gave me a rare newborn smile.

My sweet wife was now safe, the baby was healthy, and my other children were happy and healthy too. Was this a stressful time in our lives? Yes. I did my best to fulfill my duties as a spouse, father, and priesthood leader. During this time, Mandy and the children continued to support me in my duties as the bishop, and I felt "sanctified by the Spirit unto the renewing of [my body]," as stated in D&C 84:33.

Mike Chadwick; his wife, Mandy; and their six children live in Anchorage, Alaska. Mike currently serves as the stake president of the Anchorage Alaska Chugach Stake. He enjoys hiking, camping, and water-related sports.

Yea, even the wonders of eternity shall they know.

—*D&C* 76:8

Saying Good-Bye

By Eve Garnier

In 2003, my husband, John, was diagnosed with stage-three noncell lung cancer and given only one to two years to live. He went into remission, but then in October 2004, he was given about six months to live. The time came when we had to check him into the Kolob Rehabilitation Center in St. George, Utah. He had lost a lot of weight.

John was born in Cairo, Egypt, and was part French and part Italian. He was very much a Roman Catholic, and we talked about God and Jesus a lot. He tried to understand my strong Latter-day Saint beliefs, and we actually shared a deep spiritual bond.

On Monday, July 18, 2005, his last day on earth, John woke up and sat on the foot of his bed. He had been told the end was near, and he said he thought he would last until 5:30 that evening. I helped him stand up. He looked into the mirror as if it were his way of saying good-bye to his body. Then I helped him to his wheelchair, and we proceeded out to greet some of the nurses. One, our hospice nurse, Sherrie, was shocked. She had told him good-bye on Friday and had not expected to see him again.

Later, back in his room, I asked him, "Shall I call the priest?"

He said no.

"Do you want to be with me forever?"

He nodded *yes* with his head bowed. This touched me deeply.

The spirit in the room was very strong, and the nurses said ours was the most spiritual room in the hospital. During those last hours, John and I sat together, my hand on his. Finally, I kissed him on his cheek, and as I was doing that, he kissed my face and whispered, "I love you." These were the last words he would ever say to me.

The nurse came in, and together we watched him take his last breath. It was 5:35 p.m. I felt a light pressure on my hand, and when I looked down,

I could not see anything. But I knew he had touched my hand as he passed through the veil.

A year later, I was sealed to John. There are many in his family who need the gospel too, and since his passing, I have been able to submit many names to the temple.

I am grateful for that last day together. There is something sacred about the moment when someone steps away from this world into the next.

Eve Garnier has three children and thirteen grandchildren. She comes from a long line of pioneer ancestors and currently lives in Hurricane, Utah, with her daughter Krista. Eve serves as a service missionary in family history work, which she loves.

Master, the tempest is raging! The billows are tossing high! The sky is o'er-shadowed with blackness. No shelter or help is nigh.

—Hymns, *no. 105*

He Taketh . . . and He Giveth

By Carol Stewart

I had just turned eighteen when my father received a fortunate job offer a thousand miles away. My two oldest sisters had already married. That left four children to accompany our parents when they moved from our long-time home in Seattle, where our family had been well known and loved, to a town in the Midwest. We had been gone for only a few months when Dad's fragile health worsened.

His death occurred after a long, lingering illness, during which time the entire family nursed and cared for him while maintaining hope that he would eventually be cured. We had all thought that surely God would not permit *our* father to be taken from us, and we felt that our constant prayers and labors in his behalf would be rewarded in his eventual recovery. We *never* imagined that we might be expected to go on without him.

After his death, we traveled to Seattle for the funeral. A few small lines in the back pages of the newspaper were all the notice given, yet to our complete astonishment, the congregation filled not only the chapel of the meetinghouse but also the large basketball-sized cultural hall behind.

As was the custom in our area at that time, the open casket took a place of honor at the front of the chapel, and at the end of the services, his beloved family and friends were allowed to walk past for one final good-bye. When the tributes ended, I felt frozen in both time and place—I had survived the services only by exercising total self-control. I felt such overpowering emotions that I couldn't manage more than one quick look at my father as I walked past the open casket. I was beyond understanding the turmoil going on inside of me.

At that time, something curious happened to me. Somehow, my entire childhood was *blanked out*, and without fully realizing what had happened, I began my life anew without any of my childhood memories. I just went forward with my life in a state of emotional numbness, which lasted many years.

Eventually, I married and started my own family. We lived in my husband's hometown, far away from any of my former friends or family, so I had nothing, really, to remind me of my childhood days. My husband was pursuing a job in hospital administration, and he later received a job offer in Oklahoma. Our move there put me even farther away from old memories.

We were very active in the Church, and one Sunday, I found myself staring at a family that habitually sat in a bench one or two rows in front of me. The father of this family served as bishop, so while he sat in his place on the stand, his family sat facing him in the congregation.

Something about this family attracted my attention, but what? Week after week, I found myself watching his wife and six children. Strong emotion gripped me, and I would often go home from church crying without knowing the reason why. As weeks passed, I grew more and more distraught. What was happening to me? I felt myself simply falling apart. What could be wrong?

One night, I had a dream. In this dream, I saw myself walking on a path much like the one portrayed in the movie *The Ten Commandments*, where it showed the children of Israel escaping from pharaoh's army by walking through the waters of the Red Sea. In my dream, I saw myself standing on a dry path with great walls of water on each side of me, towering above my head, being held back by some mysterious force. At the top of the waters, I noticed a fierce storm whipping up large waves. I became aware that they were *very dangerous waters*, which, if this mysterious force that held them back ceased, would completely engulf and destroy me.

I was completely *alone* on this path.

At the precise moment that I noticed all of this, I heard these words, plainly spoken in my mind: *If you don't pray, you won't make it.*

The dream repeated itself three times, and after the third time, I woke up completely and knew that this was an inspired dream, that the Spirit was trying to tell me something vital to my continued existence. I started crying helplessly, and then I began praying earnestly through my tears. Thoughts and ideas flooded through me, swamping me emotionally, and I prayed with great intensity. I felt, as we sing in the hymn: "Master, the tempest is raging! The billows are tossing high!" (*Hymns*, no. 105)

For many days afterward, I continued this fervent praying. I became aware that my prayers were being answered constantly, yet I was so distressed that I feared I couldn't command my mind to be at enough peace to hear the whisperings of the Spirit.

I knew the Lord could bless us with answers, help, and guidance in many ways, and I pleaded that He would guide me to understand those things I needed to know but couldn't quite absorb because of the turmoil in my mind.

From that time forward, I found myself being taught through many means. Messages meant specifically for me were often contained in just one random sentence in a talk or on the radio or just a line in a book or magazine or newspaper—often a single line that seemed intensified and burned into my consciousness in a way that I knew it was meant especially for me. Heavenly Father was answering my prayers.

And thus the healing began. Despite the sometimes disjointed, jumbled thoughts and tearful outpourings from my soul, I became aware that the deep desires of my heart were, in fact, understood. I finally comprehended that the family I had been observing at church was *so like the one I grew up in* as to awaken, bit by bit, memories from my past. This was truly an amazing and difficult time for me. I was coming out of the prolonged numbness that had kept me in its grip for so many years.

At one point, I began to feel unaccountably suicidal. Life seemed too hard, too complicated, and I just wanted to *go home*, back to our Heavenly Father. As soon as I thought this, I felt a presence behind me that spoke quietly in my ear, "If you do this [meaning end my life], I can't help you anymore."

The very idea of losing any source of help was sobering. Someone *was* helping me, even now, and I could rely on that help continuing *as long as I didn't end my life*. I started to cry. I again remembered my dream. I was, indeed, in the midst of a storm-tossed sea and realized I needed to *be strong* and *pray* then simply walk the path that unfolded before me.

And so I did. Day after difficult day, as my mind healed, I continued on in this manner, praying earnestly and being supported by the Lord. Over time, I gradually found myself growing strong again. I knew then that "no waters can swallow the ship where lies the Master of ocean and earth and sky." By praying even when my mind felt it could hardly think and by asking for help to understand the answers I needed, I came to realize the Master was steady at the helm, and I would be safe.

Now, many years later, I can truly say, like the children of Israel, my life was saved by the direct intervention of the Lord as I walked through my own dangerous waters like those depicted in my dream, and I have been able to achieve emotional peace and a sense of well-being. I know the Lord is always there to help those who love him and turn to Him in their time of real need—that I can *never* deny. Maintaining that testimony through faith and the ability to believe has become a basic tower of strength for me, constantly supporting me through all that comes my way.

Carol Stewart is a mother of three children and thirteen grandchildren. After obtaining her degree in psychology, she worked with Child and Family Services in both Missouri and Utah for many years. With her love of music, she has had many wonderful experiences both singing and conducting choirs, including singing Beethoven's Ninth Symphony, *LeRoy Roberts'* Book of Mormon Oratorio, *and the opera* Macbeth. *Today she is developing her painting skills and enjoys being with family.*

But if it be not right . . . you shall have a stupor of thought that shall cause you to forget the thing which is wrong.

—D&C 9:9

Checking with the Lord First

By Name Withheld

I was teaching early-morning seminary some years ago when one of the senior girls became pregnant. All the other girls in the class were in awe and kind of excited about it. She was not getting married. As she got bigger and bigger with her pregnancy, the girls loved to feel the baby move, talk about baby clothes, and discuss her future motherhood. They gave her a baby shower, and the last few weeks of her pregnancy, she didn't come to seminary. At the end of the year, she brought her baby to class. The girls were so excited and oohed and ahhed over the baby. It was, indeed, a darling baby.

I started thinking that the girls really had no idea what the reality was of having a baby in your teens and having no husband. That's when I thought I would write a book about the way things *really are*. Perhaps I'd weave a story about a teenage girl in the same situation and show what really happens at home—feeding a baby every three hours and being tied down at home when your friends are out having fun. I'd try to take some of the shine and excitement out of having an illegitimate child and help my teen readers develop a more realistic understanding about life.

Two of my sisters are published authors, and I felt that I could probably take a stab at writing too. I thought a lot about it and what a service such a book would be to young girls. I knew it was a good thing to do—a righteous desire, as it were. I began to think of characters, names, personalities, and scenarios. I had the first two chapters outlined in my mind and decided it was time to start writing.

Just before I began, I decided to pray about it to know that I had the backing of the Lord in this project. I knelt and began to express my ideas, seeking the confirming Spirit. Before I got off my knees, I couldn't remember the name of the girl in my story. Then I couldn't remember the names of any of the characters or the locations or any part of my story! I was surprised and felt taken aback, as it seemed that, all of a sudden, it was just gone.

Then I remembered the scripture in Doctrine and Covenants 9:9, where it tells us that when we pray to know if a course is right, and it is not right for us, we will have a stupor of thought, causing us to forget that which is wrong. I realized that I had had a powerful answer to my prayer, and for some reason, I was not to write that book. I was disappointed, but I realized that there could be many reasons why I wasn't to write it. I'll never know, but I have never forgotten that powerful lesson to pray before beginning any important endeavor, to check with the Lord first!

But I say unto you, Love your enemies, bless them that curse you, do good to them that hate you, and pray for them which despitefully use you, and persecute you.

—*Matthew 5:44*

Turning the Other Cheek

By Name Withheld

Several years ago, I went to work for a large corporation. In many ways, it was my dream job. My children were now all in high school or college, so at the age of forty-eight, I entered the workforce again.

I loved my job, the company, and the people. There was only one problem as far as I could tell: a couple of my coworkers simply loved to gossip. No one, it seemed, was exempt—not even the people who headed the corporation. If you weren't at lunch, you were fair game, as I eventually found out.

I became so disturbed by the negative tone at lunch that I ate hastily and left. We were all Latter-day Saints, and that made it even more distressing. After about two years, I found out that this group waited for the moment when I would leave and then they would start on me.

Someone finally told me what was going on, complete with names and hurtful comments—very hurtful. My heart broke. I cried frequently for a week where no one could see. I talked to the manager about what had been going on. Trust in my coworkers' general goodwill disappeared. I wondered, were they all *really* in on this? I wanted to quit, but I had a strong spiritual impression to stay.

The manager called in everyone who had been involved. As the weeks wore on, I began to feel a chill that I hadn't noticed before. What had been done in merriment now turned mean.

When things didn't improve, the company's human rescurce department did their best to sort it out. I was assured that my coworkers had been told to lay off me completely. If they had issues with me, they were to see me privately but, at all costs, to keep it out of the lunchroom.

I began to relax. I thought with time and much kindness and forgiveness on my part, things would settle down. So I was deeply shocked at my year-end review to find out that those same ladies had been privately complaining to the manager.

The lunch group had decided there was something basically flawed about me, but they couldn't decide what. Two women assured the boss that even though they could not identify my personality problem, they were sure it existed and I was not to be trusted. Work assignments began to change.

I spoke to the manager again and expressed the destructive nature of the gossip, giving specific examples, especially about those leading the corporation. He brushed it aside as employees just letting off steam. It was normal, he assured me, and because I had been out of the workforce for so long, I didn't understand these things.

He made me feel like I was ten years old.

From that time on, I lived in fear. I began fasting and praying for long periods of time. One fast Sunday, I was alone in the house and stayed on my knees a long time pleading for insight. Answers slowly came, and I was given to understand this was an experience in *workplace emotional abuse*! I went into fresh shock. I had never heard of workplace emotional abuse. I wondered two things: Should I start keeping a record for legal purposes? And should I stand up to the women who were attacking my good name?

I received spiritual assurances on both accounts that the Lord would lead me along the best course, and my first job was not to engage with the women except in kindness and patience. I resolved to turn the other cheek and to refrain from stirring the pot in any way. Months passed as I struggled daily to keep my composure despite never-ending criticism.

One day, the manager came into my office. He was outraged. He told me that I had better shape up! He was sick and tired of all this! I had to stop it, right now!

I stared at him, shocked. I took a deep, steadying breath and asked if something had happened. Then he harshly replied, "You know better than I do, in your heart of hearts, what this is all about, so I don't need to tell you!"

He was right. I *did* know in my heart of hearts. Nothing had happened, not then, not at any other time. I pondered and puzzled, but I never did find out what was behind his outburst—the first of many. Never, however, would he tell me what he'd been told, who was saying it, or what it concerned. I could not understand why these women were so intent on their negative campaign. If I was willing to forgive and move on, why wouldn't they?

Despite constant finger pointing, no one could *ever* give me an example of unprofessional conduct. When the HR department brought us together, my supervisor told me she didn't have to give me any examples of my so-called flawed personality. And then she sneered and said, "No one could *ever* love *you*!"

I was hurt and shocked anew.

The manager assigned a new supervisor, one of my former supervisor's best friends. I wondered if I was "safe" with him. It didn't take long to find out. One day, he told me that my personality problem—whatever it was— was so offensive that I must be having marital problems. He let me know that he was just doing my husband a favor by telling me this, listed things he didn't like about me, then told me I should be grateful to him for his "insight"!

This nearly did me in. I prayed much to understand what they meant by a flawed personality. If I needed to change, well, I needed to understand in what way. Despite many, many prayers, I could not get any clear direction other than to turn the other cheek.

More than two years passed in my struggle to hang on with hope that things would improve. In that time I had been gossiped about, patronized, yelled at, shunned, lied about, and told I had an unidentifiable personality defect. I had been given the silent treatment, laughed at, made fun of, told I was not a team player by the very women who refused to speak to me; I had a supervisor fail to give me needed information to complete an assignment correctly; and I had been told I had marital problems. I was learning a lot about workplace emotional abuse.

I lived in daily fear. I rigged up a lamp to a Christmas tree timer at home and set it to turn the lamp on at 6 a.m. Then I got up at 4 a.m. every day to pray for two hours just so I could keep my heart soft, deny the adversary power over me, love my enemies, do good to those who hated me, and pray for those who despitefully used me. And I pleaded to know what I could change to find acceptance. When the lamp turned on at six, I closed my prayer and got ready to face another day of suffering.

Things got worse. A temporary worker quietly informed me that she had observed two ladies on the staff, both supervisors, who had it in for me. They often laughed and made fun of me and saw to it that people less qualified received work assignments that should have gone to me. Inside, I was crumbling. I asked myself over and over, *If all of these people see a flaw, what is it?* I sought priesthood blessings and tried hard to figure it out. My self-confidence evaporated. I really wanted to fix the problem, but I couldn't seem to find the key to do so.

My life at work eventually brought on so much anxiety that I was sleeping only about three hours a night. I found myself holding in all the hurt and heartbreak during the bus commute to the park-and-ride lot each night. But once in my car, tears poured out, and I cried all the way home. Then I wiped away my tears so my children would not worry.

In accordance with corporate policy, I finally summoned up the courage to ask for help from someone up the line. The man would not talk to me and referred me back to the HR department. This shook me deeply. I had finally run out of options. Was there *no one* to turn to who would help?

I was immediately called into a meeting on a Friday afternoon and placed on probation. I knew they had no evidence of misconduct, as I had been very careful to speak kindly, never act out, work hard, and meet all deadlines. Was this retaliation for trying to find someone to listen? I asked on what grounds this action had been taken, and I was told, "Where there's smoke, there's fire." Surely they couldn't put me on probation without some kind of tangible evidence of misconduct. Or could they?

I soon found out. They informed me of a time when I was supposedly rude to my supervisor—the same one who wanted to give me marital advice—and for this "reason," I was put on probation. I stared at this man, a Latter-day Saint, who claimed I had been rude. He had described an incident that had *never taken place*. I had *only* communicated with him about the issue in question through interoffice e-mail.

Strangely, at the time, I felt deeply impressed to make copies of that series of e-mails, which I did. I told those in the meeting that I had sent e-mails, nothing more. This was met with scorn. I wondered whether I should bring the e-mails to their attention to "prove" my innocence . . . or hold on to them. I just didn't know whom to trust.

I was at the breaking point. I knew I was not doing anything unkind or unprofessional to anyone, yet here I was on probation. The following Monday morning, I ended up in the hospital emergency room in terrible, excruciating pain. But the doctor could not find the source of it. I later learned the connection between emotional pain and physical pain. I simply could *not* go back to that workplace. He gave me a shot and sent me home. I slept for twenty-four hours. And then I went back to work.

For nearly three years, I had held on to the hope that things would somehow change, but it was not to be. At the end of my probation, I was fired. I was never given a reason based on anything I ever said or did. Evidently, the false accusations were enough—whatever they were. No one ever told me, *ever*, what made up the supposed list of accusations against me. Of course, they couldn't tell me because they consisted entirely of mean-spirited gossip.

I fell into a very dark time. I always thought that if I was kind and forgiving and followed the Spirit, the Lord would open a door. I knew the Lord knew my heart, and I later had a powerful experience in the temple confirming that I really had done *all* in my power to keep the commandments. I had a clear conscience. I had loved my enemies and turned the other cheek.

A year passed. One day, I had an idea to type "emotional abuse workplace" into my computer search engine to see what came up. Even after going through workplace emotional abuse, I didn't understand much about it other than that it had reduced me to a frightened, despairing cipher. To my surprise, a book popped up: *Mobbing: Emotional Abuse in the American Workplace*, by Davenport, Schwartz, and Elliott.

The book described bullying and harassment in the workplace, a subtle practice that targets hard-working employees in an effort to get them to leave. Suddenly, everything came into focus. According to the book, bullying often begins by one or more coworkers starting a whispering campaign to discredit another employee, usually for personal reasons. This person(s) encourages others to join with him or her to participate in continual malevolent actions aimed to force someone to quit—hence, the *hostile group becomes a mob.*

The book referred to studies and case histories of shattered careers and shattered lives. I found lists of many of the same things I'd experienced, including inappropriate joking, rumormongering, character assassination, denigration of professional contributions, withholding of information, and social isolation. As far as I could tell, we were a textbook example.

Unfortunately, individuals who experience this kind of workplace abuse usually suffer life-threatening health issues. The final chapter for nearly all came one of two ways: *termination or death,* commonly by heart attack or suicide. They had, indeed, been mobbed.

Now I began to understand what had happened, that it was more common than believed, more serious than generally acknowledged, and that my experience fit a known profile for workplace aggression. The mob reaches a point where all involved close ranks and point fingers of blame at the victim.

Why me? It is hard to know for sure. My failure to enter into the spirit of gossip was likely a factor, as was my personal work ethic. One woman told me to slow down because I was making the rest of them look bad. I didn't take her advice. Perhaps I should have.

By the time I was fired, I was emotionally and physically bankrupt. My husband was shocked at the way I had been treated. He had never seen me so broken. A doctor informed me soon after that I was on my way to serious heart problems. I was also diagnosed with post-traumatic stress disorder—my nerves were shattered. I began experiencing terrifying nightmares of a group of people chasing after me, trying to kill me. Sometimes I cried out in my sleep, begging for help. Then my husband would shake me awake and hold me in his arms.

As a Latter-day Saint, I needed a spiritual context to process this. Hadn't I acted in faith? Kept the commandments? Been worthy of a blessing? Felt impressed to stay? Hadn't I turned the other cheek?

I began to learn powerful and interesting spiritual lessons. I thought about the concept of turning the other cheek. I realized that had blessed me greatly! Knowing, nothing doubting, that I had met every criticism, every snub, every cruelty with infinite patience and calmness gave me an absolute confidence before the Lord. Spiritual peace of mind is a great asset.

Later on, I was told in a blessing that "my witness before the Lord was sufficient." As I studied about witnesses in the scriptures, I came across Alma 14 and Alma 60, both of which talk about the importance of allowing "the people [to] do this thing unto them, according to the hardness of their hearts, that the judgments which he shall exercise upon them in his wrath may be just" (Alma 14:11).

I learned that we stand as witnesses in *many* ways in this life—not only as witnesses for Christ's redemptive mission but also as witnesses for evil acts perpetrated against us. We are doing a *service for the Lord* when we go through difficult trials faithfully, giving our witnesses to Him to use in His magnificent work among men.

I also learned that the Lord knew the truth and that He would treat my sufferings with compassion and understanding. I could place my pain at his feet and receive healing. But Christ will *never* forget or marginalize or dismiss our pain. Everyone else may misjudge or misunderstand, but *He will not.*

One of the most important lessons I learned was that if I kept my eyes always on the Savior, I could not lose my testimony or "charge God foolishly" (Job 1:22) because I did not receive the outcome I had so hoped for. The Lord gives us many kinds of life experiences, and if we go through them faithfully, blessings come in unexpected ways.

I can bear a strong witness that the Lord walks with us during our trials. Without hesitation, I can say that when we are tempted to wonder *why me?* or to think God has forgotten us, *He absolutely has not.* There are many ways to stand up to forces of evil, including *simply turning the other cheek.* As we do so, our Savior will lead us to safety and sustain us through our darkest hours.

(Name Withheld) lives in the Western United States. She is pursuing new talents and finding ways to use her skills in doing good in the world. She and her husband of forty years enjoy a warm and loving home, extended family, good friends, and many sweet blessings. They recently completed a part-time mission for the Church in support of the missionary effort.

Wherefore, be not weary in well-doing, for ye are laying the foundation of a great work. And out of small things proceedeth that which is great. Behold, the Lord requireth the heart and a willing mind; and the willing and obedient shall eat the good of the land of Zion in these last days.

—*D&C 64:33–34*

A Most Unusual Arrangement

By Elinor G. Hyde

In 2005, when President Gordon B. Hinckley was ninety-five years old, the Church presented a special program featuring the Mormon Tabernacle Choir in the Conference Center in Salt Lake City. I felt compelled to attend, although it meant going downtown by myself. Despite the crowd, I was directed to a single seat near the aisle in the top balcony of the large building. As I settled into my chair, I was very impressed with the arrangement of "Come, Come, Ye Saints" (*Hymns*, no. 30) in the final rehearsal. The rendition sounded unusual, and as I listened, I realized it was being sung in unison and *without accompaniment*, perhaps as it was so often sung around the campfires of the pioneers.

Instantly, I found myself thinking of all of our many pioneer ancestors who were so faithful. We have cherished their stories, and as the music continued, tears streamed down my face. The emotions I felt seemed to honor all who had given us such a wonderful heritage. As I fumbled for tissues, the lady sitting next to me reached over and touched my hand. Her kind gesture added to my intense feelings, and I was almost sobbing as the choir ended the song that symbolizes so much of what the pioneers had endured.

The choir was dismissed for a short break before the performance was to begin, and I finally gained enough composure to apologize. I explained how I had keenly felt the spirit of our many pioneer forebears.

"Oh, it's okay. I understand," the lady said. "The feeling in this hall hit us as we entered the Conference Center. We were both in tears even before the choir began rehearsing. We're here from Orem to celebrate our fortieth anniversary with a night to ourselves."

As she added a few short details of serious health problems her husband was enduring, her voice became tender. They knew they would likely not see another anniversary. As we do so often in the Church, we each felt a bond of friendship that came from the spirit of the gospel.

I took out my small notebook and began jotting down all of the names of my pioneer ancestors. I knew our great-grandchildren were eighth- and ninth-generation descendants, but it seemed good to make a special note of that in honor of the occasion. As the program began, I eagerly awaited the actual performance of "Come, Come, Ye Saints" that had touched me so intensely. I hoped it would soon be recorded so I could share this particular arrangement with my family.

To my amazement, when the choir sang the hymn, they sang the familiar, standard version that is so popular. I was stunned. *Why not the new version they had practiced?* Quietly, I asked my new friend, "Did they not sing it differently in rehearsal?" She verified that, indeed, the choir's performance was exactly as it had been rehearsed. It was beautifully done but not unique.

I realized I had been given a precious insight and connection with the pioneers, not only those in my family but all of the pioneers. For one brief moment, I was privileged to feel the intensity of their music as they sang holy words from hearts that knew sacrifice. I felt a strong sense of gratitude and a feeling that I had represented my pioneer ancestors at that momentous concert honoring our beloved President Gordon B. Hinckley. I also seemed to experience an additional feeling of gratitude from them to me for my efforts to keep them in remembrance, both within my family and also as a member of the Daughters of Utah Pioneers.

Elinor G. Hyde is an award-winning author who has published essays, articles, poetry, stories—including a novel, Canadian Windsong *(Randall Book, 1987)—and historical data, with a chapter in* Brigham Young's Homes *(Utah State University, 2002). She credits her husband, Alan A. Hyde, with encouraging her to "learn and do it all." They are the parents of six children and have twenty-four grandchildren and twenty great-grandchildren. They have lived in the Mt. Olympus area of the Salt Lake valley for nearly fifty years, where they currently serve as stake historians and family history missionaries.*

He Is There in Times of Need

Whatsoever ye shall ask in faith, being united in prayer . . . ye shall receive.

—D&C 29:6

My Bug Story

By Bonnie Smith

It was a beautiful, bright day, and I wanted to be out playing and having fun with my five young children. I worked around the house and enjoyed watching them play outdoors through my kitchen and family room windows. My children have always entertained themselves outside with four-square, basketball, tetherball, Frisbees, hobby horse races (homemade by my husband and me), baseball, tag, the sprinklers, slip and slides with a hose and Visqueen, the jungle gym, and many games and activities they have created themselves. On this particular day, I finished my activities inside and headed out to my backyard to join in their fun.

One of our favorite family games is capture the flag. I believe this is what we were playing together that day when I suddenly felt something hit my ear. I started to hear a strange, echoing noise. The sound intensified, and it felt as though someone was stomping around in my head! A bug had somehow flown right into my ear! I was overwhelmed by the loud sounds and feeling of movement in my ear canal from this intruder.

I started running around and shaking my head, trying desperately to release the seemingly immense yet obviously tiny invader. How could one little bug cause so much havoc in my head? I looked like a crazy person as I danced a wacky zigzag pattern all over my yard. My children became a bit concerned as they watched their mother's strange behavior. No one but me could hear the deafening sound or feel the wild commotion going on in my head. No matter what I did, I could not get the thing out!

I finally ran into the house to our family room. Yelling above the internal racket in my ears, I called for my children to come quickly. I fell to my knees and beckoned my children to join me. We knelt down in a circle, and one of my girls prayed to our Father for heavenly help. She offered a simple prayer of faith, asking for divine intervention.

I stood up, and within seconds, the little bug that had caused me so much trauma walked right out of my ear and flew away! I was so thankful and relieved. The children and I all knelt down again and thanked the Lord for this miracle. We had been truly blessed in our time of need. It is a joy to not only play with my children but also to faithfully pray with them. I have no doubt that their faith and prayer caused that insect to find its way out and bring peace back to my life.

I know the Lord waits to hear from us. He desires to bless us and help us if we will but ask.

Bonnie Smith lives in Kennewick, Washington, with her husband, Sam. They have five children: a daughter in high school, one in college, one a recent graduate from a master's program, and two more who are serving missions. Bonnie enjoys her family, games, the ocean, mountains, flowers, swimming, basketball, and volleyball, as well as exploring natural ways to be healthy. Bonnie, a certified PE teacher, has been a stay-at-home mom since the birth of her first child. She teaches swimming in the summer and often teaches square dancing at school and Church activities.

The Lord hath been mindful of us: he will bless us.

—Psalms 115:12

The Inconvenient Blessing

By Stephanie Daich

While attending college, I found caring for my family was a joy, but doing housework on top of everything else was not always my favorite pastime. At times I tackled the mundane task with reluctance and boredom. I had never really stopped to think about the possibility of not even having a house to clean. What if it was taken away from me?

It was toward the end of a long day, and I really didn't want to be stuck in a classroom. I could hear birds chirping and feel the sun's rays through the window. It was the first warm day of the year, and I wanted to be outside with my children: Natalie, eleven; Emily, nine; and Robert, seven. As soon as class ended, I got into my car and sped toward our home.

On the drive home, I thought about what I wanted to do with the kids. I decided a trip to the park would be delightful. We would buy Slurpees and spend the rest of the evening relaxing and playing together.

I pulled the car into the driveway and went into the house. It was a mess. There were clothes, toys, garbage, and junk everywhere. *Oh, my poor beloved home.* Cleaning was definitely not how I had planned to spend my evening, yet it had to be done. Frustrated, I picked up a few things and carried them to the children's rooms.

As I put some things on Emily's bed, I looked at the walls. Wrapping around the room was the jungle mural I had painted. I smiled as I admired my handiwork. I had spent a huge amount of time on the mural, and it really had been a work of love.

I went back downstairs and gathered all of the clothes scattered around the front room. Carrying them into the laundry room, I noted the mural I had painted in there too. In fact, my husband and I had spent a lot of time personalizing our home. It was ours in so many special ways. As I stuffed the dirty clothes into the hamper, I felt a special peace and quiet satisfaction that my efforts had created places of caring beauty in many areas of our home.

Soon my kids walked in the front door.

"Mom," I heard them call. "We're home."

Excitedly, I scampered upstairs to meet them. All three launched themselves into my arms, and their thrust sent me to the floor, laughing. I pulled myself up gasping for breath.

"Isn't it a beautiful day?" Natalie said wistfully.

"Yes!" I said. "I think we should go to the park."

The kids jumped up and down. They loved the idea.

"If you guys can get your jobs done in twenty minutes, we'll head over to the gas station and get Slurpees to take with us."

That was all the motivation the kids needed. They immediately began working. Natalie and I headed to the kitchen, where I gathered the dirty dishes and took them to Natalie, who washed them at the sink. Next, I turned to the stove. Because there was no room on the counter, I had put the bread maker on top of the stove the night before. Since I was planning on making more bread, I left it there and simply cleaned around it.

While I was doing that, I heard a crash. I looked over at Natalie, who had thrown the last dish into the dishwasher with such startling force, it almost broke. "I'm done," she announced. "Let's go."

Robert and Emily darted into the kitchen. "We're done too! Can we go now? Can we go now?" Robert impatiently asked.

I thrust my hands into my pockets to make sure I had what I needed. "Let's go!" I declared. The house looked sweet and peaceful once again.

The children were excited as we paraded down the sidewalk toward the gas station. Our adventure had begun. They had finished their jobs in record time in order to collect their prize. As they skipped and sang, I checked my pockets one more time to make sure I had everything. Yes, it was all there.

We arrived at the gas station, and my children bolted through the front doors and hustled to the back of the store. I handed them cups and let them choose their flavor and fill the cups themselves. It only took seconds to realize the mistake I had made. Robert was the first to thrust his cup under the Slurpee spout. The cup filled, and he tried to throw back the handle, but it was too late. Blue icy fluid trickled down the cup, down his hands, and down onto the floor.

I went to grab napkins to mop up the mess. In the meantime, Natalie and Emily were making their own messes. I looked at the floor, and there was Slurpee liquid everywhere. I tossed the napkins at Natalie and told her to clean the floor. She reluctantly took them and sloppily mopped up the mess. A little embarrassed, I made my way over to the clerk.

"Sorry," I told the annoyed clerk. I could tell that we had overstayed our welcome. I reached into my pocket to grab my wallet to pay. We needed to get out of there before we made any more messes. I searched through my pockets for my wallet. I was sure I'd put it in my pocket before we'd left. Hadn't I? But where was it?

My wallet was gone. Had it fallen out? I looked at the cashier and flashed a weak grin. First the mess, and now I had to admit I didn't have my wallet. I quickly reviewed my options: I could leave the Slurpees melting on the counter and drag my kids all the way home and back, or I could dash home quickly and grab some money. I had no idea what had become of the wallet.

"I'll be back in two seconds," I said to the clerk. I turned to the children. "Wait here. I'll be right back." I was fairly sure they would be safe for a couple of minutes. As things turned out, it was a good call.

I raced home as fast as I could, achieving top speeds for me. I unlocked the front door and flew into the house—and into clouds of thick, black smoke. Stunned, I stopped. Why was my front room full of smoke? We had only left the house a few minutes earlier. I ran to the kitchen and found flames ascending around the bread maker, which was on fire and melting. The burner below was bright red. Thick, noxious smoke clouded the kitchen. Coughing, I scrambled to the stove and turned off the burner. Going to the sink, I filled a pitcher with water and drenched the blaze, putting out the flame. I stood there in disbelief, staring at the charred mess.

Somehow, the bread maker had accidentally been pushed back into the on/off knob and had turned the stove on, possibly when I was cleaning the stovetop. When I arrived, the flames had been just inches from the cupboards above the stove—and minutes from engulfing the entire kitchen in flames.

With the fire out, reaction set in. I immediately dropped to my knees as a feeling of love overpowered me. I knew my dear Heavenly Father had brought me home. I said a prayer of thanksgiving. I clearly remembered putting my wallet in my pocket before I left. And yet, when I went to pay, it wasn't there. If I hadn't had to return home to look for my wallet, I would never have discovered the fire. My kids and I would have proceeded to the park with our Slurpees while our home burned down.

Every room was saturated with thick, black smoke. I threw open all of the windows, and while I was in my bedroom, I found my wallet. I took off running all the way back to the gas station to get the children. I explained to the clerk and the children what had happened. Because the house was so smoky, we continued on to the park to let it air out.

Later that evening, when we returned, we knelt as a family and gave thanks to the Lord for preserving our dear home. I cooked dinner outside on the patio, and we stayed outside until quite late. By the time we finally went to bed, much of the smoke had cleared.

I am so thankful to the Lord for the miraculous way He blessed my family that day. At the time, I'd felt inconvenienced and annoyed by the misplaced wallet—until I understood. Our home is more than wood, nails, painted murals, and brick. It's also a place where memories are forged, bonds are created, trials endured, and families strengthened. My attitude toward housework also underwent a change. The drudgery I'd felt earlier evaporated as I experienced overwhelming gratitude for our home.

If we trust in God's infinite goodness, we soon learn that He has only the best intentions in store for our lives. I love my Heavenly Father so much and am so thankful for His hand in blessing my life.

Stephanie Daich, mother of four, lives in Brigham City, Utah. She is a nurse who has a passion for service. Stephanie has interests in many areas: family, writing, piano, guitar, dancing, outdoors, creativity, and dreaming. She believes that life should be lived to the fullest.

For I do know that whosoever shall put their trust in God shall be supported in their trials, and their troubles, and their afflictions.

—Alma 36:3

Fishing with the Deacons

By Paul Emmer

The old sheepherder was right—this was the best fishing lake in the Uintas. It seemed like with every cast, we hooked a beautiful rainbow trout. It was so exciting. I was ten years old, and this was the first real fishing trip for my eight-year-old brother and me. My father had recently been called to be the deacons quorum advisor, and this activity was to get acquainted and bond with the quorum. It turned out to be one of the most memorable events in my early youth, but not because of the great fishing.

According to one of the deacons, who seemed to be an expert in these matters, the best fishing happened to be in the Rock Creek area in the Uinta Basin, Duchesne County, Utah. The Uinta Basin is fed by creeks and rivers flowing south from the Uinta Mountains. There are many high peaks in the Uintas, including the highest peak in Utah—Kings Peak—at over thirteen thousand feet.

The drive from Salt Lake City took about three hours. We left early one summer Saturday morning—long before the sun rose. Dad drove his old 1949 Chevrolet pickup truck, the only vehicle we owned at the time. All five or six deacons, along with fishing equipment and my younger brother and me, were loaded into the open bed of the truck.

The drive seemed to take forever and included a long stretch of unpaved, dusty road that lead through hills where sheep were herded. We asked one of the sheepherders for final directions, and we were told that the best fishing was in a lake not far away. The beautiful lake was surrounded by very steep hills all the way around. He warned, however, that if it should cloud over, we must get out of the area immediately, since rain quickly turned the clay road into mud, which became almost impassable for a vehicle.

Soon we found the lake and began fishing. Everyone seemed to be having a lot of success. As the afternoon wore on, we noticed a few clouds forming above. Those clouds quickly filled the sky and threatened rain. Then the first rain drops began to fall. Dad called the boys together, and we gathered up the gear and the day's catch and loaded it all into the back of the truck.

What had begun with a few drops soon became a heavy rainfall, and the road became more and more slippery. The old pickup began to slide along the road as the wheels spun more and more and traction became difficult. As the wheel traction decreased, the truck began to move more slowly. Finally, we were not moving at all. We were stuck.

Dad tried to rock the truck back and forth to get us going again, but we seemed only to get more deeply stuck. Finally, Dad asked us to get out and push. All the deacons jumped out and began to push but to no avail. I don't know how long we labored to free the truck, but we were all wet, caked with mud, cold, discouraged, and exhausted. I was freezing. And the rain was now coming down in torrents.

Finally, after we had done all we thought we could possibly do, my dad gathered us together and said we needed help beyond ourselves. I immediately thought of the sheepherder or perhaps others in the area who might help. Then dad said we needed to bring this to the Lord and ask for His help. He asked us to kneel by the running boards of the old truck, and he offered a pleading prayer to the Lord.

I remember getting up after that prayer, and I felt a calm settle over me that all would be well. Then I heard Dad say in a confident voice, "Everyone in the truck; we're going home."

We all jumped into the truck bed again, and I remember hearing the engine rev. At first nothing happened, but then we began to move very slowly. We still slid occasionally, and there was fear of sliding off the road as we crossed over a deep embankment on one side. But finally, after what seemed like a long slog, we drove out of the basin. We made it home late that night and were greeted by worried parents.

It was a great fishing trip. We all caught our fill of fish, but the thing I will remember most is praying to the Lord in the wet and the mud and feeling that my cry for help was heard and answered. I've carried that memory with me throughout my life and have had the assurance that the Lord will help me no matter how much mud I've gotten myself into.

Paul Emmer, a graduate of the University of Utah, lives in Sandy, Utah, with his wife, Juliet. They have four children. Paul, recently retired, spent his career in the energy industry. He served for thirty-five years as an officer in the

Army National Guard and was mobilized during the Iraqi Freedom Campaign. Paul enjoys tinkering in the garage and considers himself a world-class fix-it man. Paul and Juliet plan on serving a mission for the Church. He currently serves in the Draper Temple.

*For I was an hungred, and ye gave me meat: I was
thirsty, and ye gave me drink: I was a stranger, and ye took me
in: Naked, and ye clothed me: I was sick, and ye visited me:
I was in prison, and ye came unto me.*

—Matthew 25:35–36

One Small Decision

By Name Withheld

I graduated from law school in 1992, and after going it on my own for a few years, I felt fortunate to be hired on with a larger firm. I found out later that they hired mostly inexperienced CPAs and newly degreed lawyers. After several months, my high expectations and regard for their work began to fade. By the time I'd been there a year, I was pretty sure they were up to things I didn't feel right about. Still, I rationalized that I'd be very careful, and I continued to work for them.

I gradually became aware that things were even worse than I thought, so after sixteen months, I started looking for a new job. This wasn't the place for a returned missionary and an active LDS husband and father. I found a new job and left. I loved my new firm and felt I'd made a good choice.

Then, eight months later, there was a loud knock on our front door around 10:30 p.m. on a Friday night. My wife and I were in bed eating ice cream and watching a movie. I went to the door, and a police officer held out a warrant for my arrest on securities and fraud charges. I went into shock. I absolutely did not see it coming. They took me to jail, knowing it would be Monday before I could make appropriate legal arrangements.

When I was released from jail, I went straight to my bishop and stake president to discuss with them what had happened. I followed their advice to the letter.

Five months later, I sat with the victims across a table. We talked about their financial problems and my part in them. At the end of the discussion, they informed the judge that they did not want me to go to jail, as they realized I had not been a principle player in their loss. I had made one small, unwise decision that I thought would help my client but resulted in unintentional consequences. I'd made a mistake. I agreed to contribute to their restitution fund. I certainly did not want them to suffer any losses on my account, however minor, and we all parted feeling good about the final outcome.

I thought the nightmare had ended.

A year later, in 2002, my boss called me into his office and showed me an article in the paper that said I was under indictment for tax evasion. It was the first I knew of it. I was fired on the spot. Profoundly shaken, I went home to tell my wife about this new charge. And again, I visited with my bishop and stake president.

The summer before, a new family had moved into the ward, and the husband was called as the elders quorum president. He was asked to choose counselors before he had met most of the quorum members personally. Without knowing who was who, and while I was out of town with my family, my name kept popping into his mind as he went over the elders quorum list. When he told the bishop, the bishop asked him to go back and pray about it again. He did. There was no mistake. I was called to be his second counselor.

It helped me a lot right then to know the Lord did not look upon me in the same light as I assumed the rest of the world saw me. How powerful were the words in Doctrine and Covenants 58:42, "Behold, he who has repented of his sins, the same is forgiven, and I, the Lord, remember them no more."

Besides being the elders quorum president, this new ward member also ran a business and, when he found out I was no longer with my firm, brought me in for an interview with his partner, who hired me on the spot. Over the years to come, this man whom I served with became a good friend.

Three years went by as this new charge weaved its way through various court proceedings. It was stressful, but I felt I would weather this too. Suddenly, one Friday afternoon, I got a call at 4:30 from the prosecuting attorney. "You need to plead guilty. Now! Otherwise we'll prosecute you to the fullest extent."

Plead guilty? *Plead guilty?* I had expected some way to work it out, just as I had before. I had one day to decide. My wife and I spent most of that night in prayer and long discussions together. By morning, we both had, independently of each other, received a strong spiritual witness as to the best course to take.

I contacted the prosecutor and pleaded guilty. The spiritual witness I'd had that night had been undeniable. That strong witness would carry me through a long and painful journey. Later, I came to understand that the federal government was looking for someone to create news headlines about tax evasion—during April. Now I had my name in the paper again, and I had to live with that public humiliation.

Eight months later, I was sentenced to twenty-nine months in federal prison. This shocked everyone, especially me. It had been generally assumed that because my part had been so minor, I'd be warned and given a suspended sentence. Maybe pay a fine. But suddenly I faced going to prison. It was unbelievable! How had *this* happened?

That night I did one of the hardest things I'd ever had to do in this life: I sat down with my two sons, both under ten, and told them I had made a very small mistake a few years ago, and it had now resulted in a very large consequence. I come from a family who seldom shows emotions, but that night, all constraints went out the window. We cried and cried together.

My last Sunday at church in my home ward, the bishop came into the Gospel Doctrine class and said that I had made a mistake but had done all that was required of me from the gospel perspective (and I had), and now I had to pay a price to society. Then he asked ward members to be careful how this was discussed around their children—my sons' friends. He asked them to put their arms around my family and help them weather this crisis.

I can say that my ward not only gave my wife and children support during this time, but they also gave me love and support as several people made it a point to write to me during the coming months. I volunteered to enter prison early, and I was sent to a nearby jail for three months, then to Oklahoma for a week, and finally to a prison two states away from my family.

I faced many new challenges. One that weighed heavily on me was how to best help my sons grow toward manhood. How would I counsel my boys to stay out of trouble? It was clear I needed to think that one through.

I realized that one of the first things I had to do was forgive the zealous prosecutor for choosing me to send a warning to the legal community in my city. I had to put aside bitterness and show my boys that even under the worse possible conditions, a loving Father in Heaven will sustain and carry you through your trials. It took about five months, but I was able to find peace about what had happened.

I set about finding ways to create something positive from the experience. I spent most of my free time reading. I found a full set of scriptures in the prison library and spent about four hours a day studying the sacred words I had loved since I was a small boy. As I read, I wrote out questions about gospel topics and made in-depth notes about verses that shed light on the questions I had raised. My understanding of the gospel deepened considerably. In addition, I decided to read all of the books on the masters of English literature list from two major universities. My brother was very kind to me and sent me a new book from the list every week, so by the time I was released, I had improved my understanding of English literature.

As is not uncommon in the Church, a nearby stake provided Sunday services at the "camp" (aka, prison for white collar crimes, no bars) for anyone who wished to attend. They had formed a small LDS branch with a two-hour block that I attended every week. I met another Latter-day Saint, this one a returned missionary from Italy. Since I had served in Mexico, we decided that he would teach me Italian and I would teach him Spanish. We spent time every day reading a chapter or two from the Book of Mormon first in one language, then the other, each of us correcting the pronunciation of the other. At the end of two years, I had become fairly fluent in Italian.

Perhaps two of the most important things I did were spend a lot of time in prayer and give service. We lived in what could only be described as cubicles within a large gymnasium-type room. The walls were about five feet high, and there were no doors. And no privacy. I would sit on my bunk bed as if resting and pray for long periods of time.

As I looked around, I realized there were many men there who had no one on the outside to give them support. I began to reach out. I decided I would be a friend to them. This became a rich opportunity to lift spirits and share my belief in God. We were not allowed to proselytize, but I shared my testimony anyway.

In a more practical manner, I also shared some of the "bounty" I got from the commissary. Families were allowed to send a little money each month that we could use to buy things we needed. My family sent the full amount allowed, so I would buy ingredients from the commissary and prepare creative meals and snacks with my only cooking tool: a common room microwave oven. It was these meals I shared with some of the men who had no one sending them anything from the outside.

But the highlight of my day was always the ten-minute call I made nightly to my home. I spoke with my sons and my wife every day. I tried not to complain but used the time to build faith and gospel understanding in my boys. In addition, my family made the long trip to see me several times, as did other family members. I was fortunate to have a strong, loving extended family behind me.

Each of us in the camp had a job to do. My first was cleaning bathrooms. Later on, I became a baker, and within six weeks, I was made head baker. This meant getting up at 3:30 a.m., and after a few months, my health began to suffer. I could not go to bed early because of the noise and lights that stayed on until 10 p.m. each night, so I finally relinquished this highly desirable job despite many protests from the other inmates who liked my baking.

Next, I became a teacher, working with men with poor English skills. I taught ESL classes and helped them become more proficient in English. My class had native Spanish, Arabic, and Chinese speakers, and I enjoyed finding ways to make creative lessons that would help them improve their English. I spent about one year teaching and thoroughly enjoyed helping these men learn and improve their language skills.

Sundays, however, I did not work. I made a point of getting up very early and going outside to sit on a bench with my scriptures and watch the sunrise. After I had been away from my family for almost nine months, it came time for another general conference. After careful discussion with the prison administration, we were informed that this time, Latter-day Saints would be allowed to go to a nearby chapel to watch the Sunday sessions under close observation of staff who went with us.

When I walked into the chapel foyer and looked upon a painting of the Savior, I was overcome with an all-pervading feeling of His love. The building, artwork, furniture, and carpet were so familiar, so comforting. I felt the same spirit I experience when I walk into a temple. I had come home.

Not only were we allowed to watch conference on those days, but we were also given the most remarkable meal between sessions by dear Relief Society sisters—in some ways the best meals I've ever eaten. I never felt judged by these wonderful women, only loved. Included in this group were the wives of the branch presidency. These sisters showed us the same care and concern I had received from the wife of my mission president so many years ago. In short, they loved me like I was their son.

The day came when I was finally sent to a halfway house near my home. It was Christmastime, but they would not allow me to go home for even a few hours. Still, it marked the closing scenes of this most difficult and unexpected journey. Finally, I was released.

My first Sunday back in my home ward, I felt awkward. What do you say to people? I needn't have worried. I could hardly take a step without someone stopping me to shake my hand, give me a hug, and welcome me home. In fact, other than the friends and family at my wedding reception, I'd never in my life had so many people greet me with so much love.

There were many lessons I took from this experience. Some were very simple, such as, "I was in prison, and ye came unto me." People with kind and loving hearts made a difference. Other spiritual lessons included a firm and unyielding testimony that our Heavenly Father loves us and cares deeply about our mortal journey. He supports us in our trials, and as I used so much of my time in gospel study, I had grown in countless ways.

Yes, it has been difficult, embarrassing, humiliating, and very awkward at times. I have had to keep my focus strictly on our Savior, who knew my heart and understood it all. He did not judge me but lovingly opened doors for me along a most difficult journey. I love Him. I am grateful to Him for helping me find good in the midst of what might have been a dark and difficult journey.

(Name Withheld) went back to school for training in a new field and is now working once again. His boys have become fine, good young men, with their testimonies intact. His wife, who has supported him throughout the long journey, is still his best friend. He serves once more in the elders quorum presidency in his home ward.

Wherefore, whoso believeth in God might with surety hope for a better world, yea, even a place at the right hand of God, which hope cometh of faith, maketh an anchor to the souls of men.

—Ether 12:4

A More Excellent Hope

By Shirley Manning

Death can be an especially frightening prospect for one who does not have the comforting reassurance that a loving Heavenly Father waits for His children to return to a heavenly home after mortality. This was the uncertainty my sister Nancy faced as she contemplated the diagnosis of her oncologist, who wept as he told her that she had a year, maybe a little more, to live.

Nancy instinctively reached a hand of comfort to her doctor and wondered at her own words. "Don't worry," she said. She later told me how unreal that conference with him had seemed.

The stunning diagnosis, "inoperable brain cancer," didn't exempt Nancy from miserable radiation treatments and chemotherapy to extend her life by precious and perilous increments—increments that gave her afternoons to frame beautiful Gig Harbor, Washington, through her picture windows. Her view included a little concrete lighthouse that welcomed seagulls all day and spread its light over the dark water all night.

For many years, Nancy chose not to believe in God. She had an innate kindness and spirituality that she found voice for in nature. She observed the grandeur and the peaceful quietude of a beautiful world as she enjoyed outdoor activities with her family—cross-country skiing, hiking, mountain climbing in the majestic Cascades, and sailing in the incomparably beautiful Puget Sound.

At this time in her life, though, she was not able to enjoy those activities any longer or the solace that they had brought to her. She suffered from seizures and periodic sickness as she followed the chemotherapy schedule. She had difficulty walking at times because of dizziness and difficulty talking because of the location of the growing tumor in her brain.

I could only imagine what it must be like for her without the reassuring anchors of the gospel. I prayed that she might remember the merciful truths she had been taught as a child—that God exists and loves her as His daughter and that there is a real life after this one.

Her husband, daughter, and son tenderly cared for her as the months streamed inevitably by. Friends and family came miles to visit and spend the passing days with her, often sitting in her comfortable living room, looking out her windows at the harbor.

As she grew weaker, Nancy's family and friends were given a time limit to spend with her. It seemed unreal to us. It was hard to cram what should have been many years of time spent together into a few fleeting visits. I remember with special fondness one visit I and my sister Karen made to see Nancy. We traveled in an SUV filled with family heirlooms, genealogy papers, and photographs that our mother, who had recently died, had laid aside for Nancy.

On a clear May afternoon, the three of us sat on Nancy's overstuffed leather couch, alternately squinting through a small plastic viewer at Kodak slides of our childhood or looking out the huge windows at the multichromatic beauties of Puget Sound. We laughed at stories the slides recalled and teased one another about the dumb things we had done as kids.

Sometime in our conversations, we broached the subject of death, which we would rather have avoided. Though religion had not been something we had discussed for many years, I told Nancy of the Father in whom I believed and the heaven where He lived and that He had prepared a place for her to come.

I so wanted her to have that "more excellent hope" in which I believed—that there really was a "house prepared . . . among the mansions of thy Father" (Ether 12:32)—so she could be comforted and look forward with a lighter heart to a marvelous, loving home that surely awaited her, where she would be with family members who had gone before.

Silence soon fell over our geniality as Nancy succumbed to exhaustion, falling asleep on the couch, as she did most afternoons. Karen and I sat close by and talked quietly as she rested. After a while, she woke suddenly and sat up.

"She touched my shoulder," Nancy said. "The angel touched my shoulder."

Nancy's earnestness brought us both to her side, and we took her hands in ours.

"It was like the angel from *The Little Match Girl*," she said.

Nancy's words were coming out pretty well right then. She explained to us, as we filled in a word here and there with her nodding approval, that *The*

Little Match Girl was the favorite story she read to her children every year at Christmastime. She knew and loved that story. Because her family didn't read scriptures, I believe that story may have been her only frame of reference for things beyond the veil.

Her eyes were soft and believing, shining with tears and wonder. "In my dream, I sensed that everything would be okay," Nancy said. "I felt so loved and comforted that it seemed real. Do you believe me?" she asked.

"With all my heart," I said.

I thought that she had felt the powerful influence of the Holy Ghost testifying to her that everything would be okay. I knew that the comforting spirit of our loving Heavenly Father could be expressed in meaningful ways to each of us. I have felt that Spirit testifying to truths and reassuring me of the very existence of God and of His Son Jesus Christ.

I believe Nancy's experience gave her the reassurance she needed to truly hope for a home in heaven, lovingly prepared by her Father. There were not many precious days left to spend with Nancy before she passed away. I have often recalled that sunny afternoon spent with her, and I have been amazed at how kind Heavenly Father is to speak peace to each one of us in a language we can understand.

Shirley Manning resides in Kaysville, Utah, with her husband, Marty. They feel blessed to live close to their extended family, including fifteen grandchildren, and they all visit one another often.

Pray always, and I will pour out my Spirit upon you, and great shall be your blessing.

—D&C 19:38

Blessing Baby Derek

By Michael Hacken

I was in the anatomy lab at the University of Louisville School of Dentistry on a Friday afternoon in February, preparing for a demanding midterm test that would be given the following Monday morning. Our head-and-neck anatomy class was considered by many students to be the most difficult class of our first year. When I was nearly finished reviewing for the day, I checked my phone and discovered I had missed a call from my wife, Tiffani. I listened to my voice mail message from her right away.

Our baby, Derek, only seven months old, had been sick and struggling to breath, and Tiffani had decided to take him to the pediatrician. I could hardly understand what she was saying through her sobbing, but I did get the chilling words, "They're taking Derek by ambulance to the Kosair Children's Hospital downtown." Could I meet them there?

Worry coursed through my veins like ice water. Fortunately, the dental school was only two blocks away from the hospital. I had a good LDS friend, Josh, also a dental student in my class, who was with me in the lab that day. I asked him if he could come with me to the emergency room. We left the lab together and rushed to the hospital. The next few hours became a nightmare of worry.

When we arrived, I found Tiffani holding our baby in a small, private room off the emergency room. Little Derek was still having a hard time breathing. My heart was filled with love for the little guy. I don't think I realized just how much I loved him until I saw him in the emergency room of the hospital. I knew my son needed help right away. I had previously given a few priesthood blessings to my children, but never had I been faced with anything this serious.

Josh and I waited for the doctors and nurses in the emergency room to leave. I was relieved to have a friend with me who had consecrated oil with him and who was able to help me give Derek a blessing. My heart cried out for healing for my young son. Was my faith sufficient? Would I even feel inspired? Was I prepared and worthy? Would the Lord bless him to be healed? Would the Lord help a young father who was nervous and inexperienced?

Josh anointed, and I sealed the anointing. Although I don't remember the exact words said during the blessing, I still recall the spirit of peace that entered the room, and I knew Derek would be all right. I had done my best to be open to the will of the Lord, and I felt greatly comforted by the deep peace that accompanied the words I spoke over my son's head. I was glad I felt worthy to give a blessing that would help my sweet little baby boy.

Tiffani was still nursing Derek, so we had to arrange babysitters for our other two children so she could stay at the hospital. I went home to pick up the kids later that night and took them back to our house. They didn't know what was going on and were a little upset at the sudden change in their routine.

Until Derek could get enough oxygen, he had to stay in the hospital, so I had to go back and forth between home and hospital to help Tiffani and to take care of our other children. Time to study for the big test on Monday was going to be hard to find.

I called my mother in Utah with the bad news and asked her to fast and pray for us, and I also asked her to call my sisters to tell them what was happening. Mom mobilized the entire family, and they all fasted and prayed for Derek to recover, for me to pass my test, for Tiffani, and for our other children.

The next day was Saturday. Normally, I would have been at the library all day long studying for the big test on Monday, but with Derek and Tiffani at the hospital and our other kids upset, I knew I wouldn't be able to study very much. Tiffani found a babysitter so I could try to get in some study time. Before I went to the library, I stopped at the hospital to see how Derek was doing. Even though the doctors had given him a breathing treatment, Derek still struggled. When I saw the little mask on his face, I felt sorry for him, and I couldn't help but wonder if he would be okay. I had hoped that we could bring him home, but his oxygen levels weren't high enough, so I left him there with Tiffani and continued on to the library.

I worried about Derek, but in the back of my mind, I also worried about the test. I really wanted to pass the test with a good grade. I wanted to do well in my classes to keep my options open for possible specializing.

But how could I concentrate while my small son struggled? I spent most of the weekend watching for any small sign of improvement, and when Derek finally started responding to treatment Saturday evening, we were all relieved.

We were able to bring him home that evening with strict instructions. He was, and still is, very vulnerable to any kind of respiratory illness, and we were told that complete recovery could take months, so we were not to take any chances with him.

Monday morning came, and I had not prepared nearly enough for the anatomy test. But I had prayed and done my best to study after I put the kids to bed in the evenings, and I knew that I couldn't have done any more. I also knew that Derek's well-being was the most important thing to me and that taking care of him had to come first.

I took the test and hoped for the best, but it was harder than I expected—not a good sign.

When I got my test score back a few days later, I was astounded. I not only passed, but I received a 92 percent, good enough to earn an A on the test. It was an answer to prayer and a tender mercy from the Lord. I knew that with the limited amount of study time I'd had that weekend, I could not have passed merely on my own efforts. The Lord really understood the needs of a desperate father. I had been given help to achieve far beyond my own capacity.

I am grateful that the Lord knows and loves each of us, especially tiny babies and busy parents. I am also grateful for prayer and the power of the priesthood that can heal and comfort both body and soul.

Michael lives with his wife, Tiffani Hacken, in Crestwood, Kentucky, where Michael is a second-year dental student. Today Derek still has sensitive lungs, but overall, he is in good health and is a robust, active baby.

But behold, he did deliver them because they did humble themselves before him.

—Mosiah 29:20

River Rescue

By Gina Shelley

One of my earliest memories of my father was when he decided to take my older brother, Steve, and me on a camping trip in Utah. I was about six years old, and my older brother was eight. We lived in Las Vegas, Nevada, and enjoyed any reason to escape the heat for the cool mountain breezes and beautiful scenery. We packed my father's tiny Ford Courier pickup truck with our camping gear, and the three of us squeezed into the front of the small cab.

My father was the typical kind of guy who did not ask for directions, did not always need a map, and preferred to "boondock," which translated into choosing an obscure road and then driving for miles and miles on it just to see where it ended up. As kids, we hated it when Dad wanted to take us boondocking because we never knew how long we were going to be stuck in the car, if we were going to blow a tire in a pothole, or just get plain lost! This particular camping trip was no different.

Once we arrived in the mountains, Dad discovered a dirt road he wanted to explore. It was not very long after we left the main highway before we encountered a river that the road seemed to go through. There was no bridge. Dad had the option to either forge ahead or go back and find another road that would lead us to the ideal camping spot. You can probably guess that he decided to forge ahead.

Dad had no idea how deep the river was, and because it didn't look too menacing, he put the truck in gear and slowly began to enter the water. What we did not realize was that the river's current had washed out the center of the roadbed below the surface of the water. Instead of leveling out, the road suddenly dropped us deeper into the river. I started to panic as water came in through the floorboard, and I said, "Dad! Go back! We are going to sink!"

"No, we're not. Quiet down and let me get us out of here," he said.

After a few more minutes, with the water steadily creeping up, my brother and I started shouting again. "Dad! Get us out of here!"

By then, my brother and I had our legs curled up in our arms, trying to keep our feet dry, with poor results. Dad put the pickup truck into reverse, but nothing happened. We couldn't move backward at all. He then thought he would put it in gear and try to gun it forward to get to the other side—to no avail. Neither option worked! We were completely stuck in the center of the river. As a six-year-old, disaster seemed imminent. Would the current carry us downstream? It wasn't really that deep, but at the age of six, it looked dangerous to me.

Dad climbed out the window, not daring to open the door. Standing in the freezing water, he helped us climb out the window too. I nervously stuck my head out and, with dad's help, stepped around to stand inside the bed of the truck. Soon my brother joined me. Moving to the edge of the truck bed, we jumped as far as we could toward the bank, but we both landed in the very shallow water near the edge and had to scramble out to dry land.

"Go up to the highway and try to flag down some help," Dad hollered as he tried to steady the truck.

The sun was beginning to set, and we knew we would not have much time until it was completely dark and we would find ourselves in more serious trouble. Cold, wet, and scared, Steve took my hand, and we walked back up the dirt road to the highway. We did not have any flashlights and had no idea how to flag down help—not to mention that the highway was not a busy one. Nobody passed for several minutes.

When Steve and I saw a car coming, we began to jump up and down, waving our arms in the air and screaming. The car got closer and closer, but it did not slow down and soon passed us by. Discouraged, we tried again and again while the sky turned darker and darker. Very few cars passed us, and each one either did not see us or simply waved back. I asked my brother if we could kneel down and offer a prayer for help. Steve agreed that it was a good idea, and we both began to pray our little hearts out.

After we finished, we stood up, and I felt a sense of peace and hope inside me.

Steve smiled at me and said, "Let's try again."

It was only a few minutes later, in near total darkness, that a large, white truck approached. Again, Steve and I began to scream, wave our arms, and jump up and down to get the driver's attention. To our relief and joy, the truck pulled over. A man got out, wearing a Scout uniform, and asked us what was wrong and where our parents were. We told him our father was down the road with his pickup truck stuck in the middle of the river and that he had sent us up here to get some help.

The man introduced himself and said he was from a local Boy Scout camp nearby. He asked us to take him to our dad, and we did. I remember how happy my father was to see that we had brought some help. The two men decided they would take us children up to the camp to drop us off, get some food, and find a place to sleep so we could be safe, and then they could get some more help to tow the pickup truck out of the river.

Once Steve and I arrived at the Scout camp, we were given dinner and a warm place to sleep for the night. I don't remember anything else from that camping trip with my dad and brother, but what I have never forgotten is that Heavenly Father answered our prayers. I became aware that night that when I really needed assistance, and prayed for it, the Lord had sent help. In the dark of that night, when no other driver noticed my brother and me standing by the side of the road, we prayed deeply sincere prayers, and we were rescued.

Gina Shelley grew up in Las Vegas, Nevada. She earned degrees at both Brigham Young University and the University of Utah. Married with four children, Gina is a professor at a university in Iowa. She loves literature, crafting, and reading. She also loves to travel and spend time with family and friends.

And because he hath done this, my beloved brethren,
have miracles ceased? Behold I say unto you, Nay; neither have
angels ceased to minister unto the children of men.

—Moroni 7:29

I Needed Help Quickly

By Barbara Anderson

Monday morning, June 22, 2008, my husband, Bryan, and I packed the camp trailer and headed to a campground in Fish Lake National Forest, located in Central Utah, for a week of fishing and fun with a few of our neighbors. On Tuesday morning, I entered my neighbor's trailer to invite her to go walking, and as I turned to leave, I missed the first step and fell from their fifth-wheel trailer, hitting the hard ground. I thought, *I've broken something*! I didn't tell anyone. But something didn't feel right, and I felt both pain and nausea.

A neighbor held out his hand and said, "Here, I'll help you up." I worried that if I got up too quickly, I might be sick in front of everyone. I had already embarrassed myself by falling. Then I realized I really couldn't get up on my own. A couple of the women in camp helped me up very slowly and got me into a chair. After awhile I was able to stand up, but I could not walk.

When my husband came back from fishing, I explained what had happened. Bryan gave me a priesthood blessing, and in that blessing, I was told that my recovery could be long but I would recover. He drove me to the hospital an hour away in Richfield, Utah, to get things checked out.

The doctor looked at the x-ray of my pelvis and assured us there were no broken bones, only damaged muscles and tendons. He told us they would recover in a few weeks and to just take it easy. He gave me a set of crutches, prescribed a pain killer and muscle relaxers, and sent us on our way.

I continued in pain, so the Monday following our camping trip, I went in to see my primary-care physician. She took another x-ray and found that I actually had broken my pelvis. No wonder I was still in so much pain! My primary-care doctor told me to continue with the medications and to be very careful not to fall and to stay down as much as possible.

About two weeks later, on July 18, I felt a bit odd when I woke up, but I didn't know why. I showered as usual, but I had a hard time getting dressed.

I was far too exhausted. When a couple of neighbors called to chat, I had a hard time even talking on the phone.

My neighbor brought dinner to the house that evening and asked if she could serve up a plate for me. I said I wasn't feeling well and asked her to just leave the food on the counter. About fifteen minutes later, I realized I didn't want anything to eat at all. I decided to get up and put the food in the refrigerator.

Using my crutches, I stood, but I immediately started breathing rapidly and couldn't seem to catch my breath. I noticed I was perspiring heavily, had a rapid heartbeat, and felt dizzy. Gripping my crutches, I carefully made my way down the hall to wash up before putting dinner in the fridge. Then, as I crossed the family room, I decided to sit down on the couch for just a few minutes to rest. I was sure the symptoms would go away. Because the couches were quite soft, I had not sat on any of them since I'd broken my pelvis. I was afraid I wouldn't be able to get up again.

As soon as I sat down, I knew I was in trouble. I couldn't move. Worse, my dizziness and rapid breathing did not go away, and I had a strong feeling that *I needed to get help quickly.*

"I need to get off this couch and walk to the phone and call Bryan. Something is really wrong, and I need to get to the emergency room," I said out loud.

Bryan worked about four minutes from home and could come quickly.

Over my shoulder, I heard a voice say, *Get your crutches, and we will help you.* I reached over, picked up the crutches, and cautiously worked my way to the edge of the couch. There, I could feel someone *lift me up.* I don't even remember walking to the chair where the phone was located.

As soon as I sat down, I called Bryan at work and told him that something was really wrong with me and that I needed to get to the hospital quickly. Bryan asked me what was happening, and I said I didn't know. Please, please hurry home.

When he walked into the house, he took one look at me and knew immediately that I was in trouble. He headed to the garage, pulled the car out front, and came back for me. "Can you walk to the car?"

Sure I can walk, I thought, but aloud I said no.

Bryan couldn't carry me, so he asked again. "Can you walk to the car?"

Again, I said no. In my mind, I was thinking, *Yes.* So why was I saying no? I didn't move from the chair, and I was getting more and more lethargic. I could hardly think any longer, yet I did not want to get into the car.

I remember hearing Bryan say, "No. It's my wife."

Who is Bryan talking to?

"No, I don't hear any sirens yet," I heard him say.

Why would we hear sirens? I thought. Then, all of a sudden, I heard them.

Suddenly, there were four firemen in my family room asking me questions. I heard the paramedic say, "Let's get the oxygen. Her level is eighty-three. Let's do an electrocardiogram."

The paramedics were surprised to see that I was skipping a heartbeat every three beats. They asked me to walk to the stretcher and lie down. Once I was in the ambulance, the paramedic tried to put an IV in me. He must have tried ten or twelve times but could not get it in.

"We're taking you to the hospital because you're having a panic attack," the paramedic said. "This isn't an emergency, so we'll drive slowly. When we get to the hospital, the doctors will give you some medication, and you'll be back home in an hour or so."

When we got to the hospital, the nurse came into the cubicle to set up equipment then went to get the doctor. Another nurse was trying to get an IV started, but she was not successful either. Finally, the doctor came in, asked a few questions, and left. He went to my family in the waiting room and told them he thought I had pulmonary embolisms, or blood clots, in my lungs and needed a CAT scan to find out.

My family was able to come back to my room. The nurse came in and said she was going to give me a shot of Heparin to start thinning my blood. I was the sixth person in line to receive the CAT scan, and each scan took about twenty to thirty minutes.

Waiting for the Heparin to start working, I was really cold. My daughter kept getting blankets from the warming oven, and when I had about ten blankets piled on me, I finally felt warm enough. Then, all of a sudden, the Heparin started to work, and I was hot, just as the doctors explained to us would happen.

All of a sudden I couldn't take the heat. "Get the blankets off! I'm really hot."

Everyone in the room started to laugh.

It was finally my turn to have a CAT scan. The orderly took me down to the room and set me up. In the middle of the scan, I heard the radiologist say to the orderly, "Go get Doctor Beard, fast!"

Doctor Beard came in, looked at the scan, then told the radiologist to finish quickly and get me back to my room. Soon Dr. Beard came in and said my lungs and heart were full of little blood clots. He told me I had hundreds of these clots in my lungs and that at least two large clots had gone through my heart and settled in the top of my lungs, which had prevented the smaller clots from leaving my lungs and traveling to my brain. If the clots had gone to my brain, I would have had a stroke. Dr. Beard called upstairs to consult with the pulmonologist.

The pulmonologist came down to my room and told me about the clots, and I asked her what it all meant. She told me the clots were severe, and I would have a long recovery. The doctor seemed surprised that I was comprehending what she was saying. Because I was asking questions, she felt that I might be all right. I was told that I would be in the intensive care unit for at least five days and in a normal room for another five days before I would be well enough to go home.

I was taken to the ICU just after midnight. The nurse told my family the staff would take good care of me so my family could go home, get some rest, and come back the next morning. The nurse also said that if anything changed, the staff would call.

After I was settled in my room, the nurse told me I needed to get some sleep. They had told us I had only about a 50 percent chance to live, and I was afraid that if I fell asleep, I would not wake up. I lay there waiting for morning to come.

The next day, they completed an ultrasound on my leg, and the test showed that I had a blood clot that stretched from my lower calf to my upper thigh. Small portions had evidently broken off, causing the existing trouble. The doctors decided that a filter needed to be put in the artery to catch any clots that might break off and explained that my heart and lungs couldn't handle one more clot. I prepared myself for a long stay.

Two days later, I was surprised when the nurse came into my room and told me I was well enough to be moved from the ICU to a normal hospital room. Then, just two days later, the pulmonologist and cardiologist came in to tell me I could go home. They both said they couldn't believe I was healed enough to leave already. They both called me their miracle patient and explained that, technically, because the clot was so severe, I should not be alive.

I went home on Wednesday afternoon. I had been in the hospital only five days.

I credit this to the help I received that day in my family room, when I thought I was alone, and also to the strange insistence I had made to not get into the car, forcing Bryan to call for an ambulance. I later found out that had I walked in, I would have had to wait several hours to be seen, and that would likely have been fatal.

My pelvis healed, and the blood clots finally dissolved. I am grateful that the Lord sent help at a very critical time and guided events in such a way as to preserve my life. The words of the priesthood blessing my husband gave me came true. It took a long time, but I did recover, and I can once more find joy in life.

Barbara Anderson and her husband, Bryan, live in Riverton, Utah. They are the parents of one daughter and two sons and the grandparents of eight wonderful grandchildren. In her spare time, Barbara loves reading, traveling, camping, quilting, serving in Church callings, and spending time with her children and grandchildren.

Trust in the Lord with all thine heart; and lean not unto thine own understanding. In all thy ways acknowledge him, and he shall direct thy paths.

—*Proverb 3:5–6*

The Almost Accident

By Frances Hatch Pershing

One winter night, the snow came down heavy and wet. I was working a second shift at a check-printing business and worked until midnight. I had to drive down a dark, narrow road to get to the main road that led to my home, and at midnight, there were no street lights, no traffic, and what few houses existed along the road were all dark.

The snow fell so thick and fast that it was hard to see where I was driving. We had an old car, and the windshield wipers only worked sporadically, leaving patches of slush and ice streaked across the window. I had to look out the side window just to make sure I was still on the road.

Then the wipers zipped across the windshield, clearing it completely—just in time for me to see I was heading directly toward the side of the road and the edge of a small bridge over an irrigation stream. I yanked the steering wheel at the last second and got myself back into my lane.

If the wipers had worked as they had been doing, moving slowly and only occasionally across the windshield and then not even clearing it, I would have crashed into the bridge and landed in a ditch in the middle of a blizzard. Because of the late hour and dark street, I don't think anybody would have heard or seen me.

As I caught my breath and steadied my car on the bridge to continue on my way home, I thought of how that morning I had prayed, as I do daily, for the Lord's watchful care to keep me safe from harm. I know Heavenly Father was watching over me that night, and I am very thankful that I got home safely to my family.

Frances Hatch Pershing graduated from Rock Springs High School in Wyoming in the dark ages (1949). She later moved to Tooele, Utah, and eventually settled in Granger, Utah, before moving to Arizona. In 2005, Frances moved to Greensboro, North Carolina, to be close to her daughter and her family.

*Know thou, my son, that all these things shall give
thee experience, and shall be for thy good.*

. . . Thy days are known, and thy years shall not be numbered less.

—*D&C 122:7, 9*

Sustained through Suffering

By Sandy Wallace

For years, I was always on the run like every other Latter-day Saint woman—wife, mother, grandmother, PTA volunteer, Primary president, counselor in most organizations in the Church, and provider of service in many other Church callings. I took meals in, bottled fruits and jams, worked in my yard, did family history work, wrote a couple of cookbooks, and attended the temple. My parents were in their nineties, so I split my time between my husband, Jack, tending grandchildren, and driving sixty miles every other day to take care of my parents. The days were fulfilling and long, and I often came home just in time to crawl into bed, exhausted.

My patriarchal blessing states that I will have problems come along my pathway of life but to be patient and have courage, faith, hope, and love in God's plan. I felt like I already had experienced my share of major problems. Little did I know there was yet another mountain to climb.

In February 2009, I began to feel severe pains in my back. After four months of constant pain, I finally went to a doctor. He listened to my symptoms and said he thought I was depressed. I told him I was stressed, not depressed, but he gave me a prescription for depression anyway—and I didn't fill it. He told me I had probably pulled a muscle in my back and said to exercise more. The entire visit took eight minutes. I walked out frustrated, even furious.

I tried to continue my busy life, but the pain forced me to lie down constantly. After two months of feeling totally worthless, I called another doctor and begged for an appointment. He agreed to stay late one night, and he examined me in-depth for forty minutes. He sent me for x-rays, and then he called to tell me he had scheduled an MRI for Saturday.

After the MRI, the nurse called to make a follow-up appointment to go over the results. I thought he was going to tell me I had osteoporosis. But the words that came out of his mouth were a total shock. I had cancer! And I might have only a couple of months to live, maybe less.

I drove home numb. *How do I wrap up my life in such a short time? Weeks fly by like days, and months whiz by in a blink of an eye. How will I get my genealogy histories and books that I'm working on completed? Who is going to take care of my husband, my parents, my children, and my grandchildren?*

Salty tears flowed down my cheeks as I formulated how I would tell my husband this news that would change our lives forever.

We shed many tears, and he said he would gladly take it from me if he could. He called a dear friend in our stake presidency, who came and gave me a beautiful blessing. He blessed us to know the Lord was very mindful of us and loved us. He said we would feel very confident in the doctors we chose and to follow their counsel. He also said the Lord would be with us throughout the trial because He loved us very much.

Every day was filled with doctors and doctor appointments, tests, questionnaires, physician assistants, and nurses. When I arrived for my appointments, I was sometimes in so much pain that they took me to the back to lie down. I began daily radiation treatments, and after each session, I would go take care of my elderly parents. In this way, I passed beyond the initial two-month window and began to hope.

I didn't think life could get much harder until my brother called one morning at six and said that both Mom and Dad had fallen trying to help each other, but only Mom was on her way to the emergency room in an ambulance. I drove to the hospital forty-five minutes away. Mother had a broken hip, and I had to find a surgeon. I was in a panic as I knew no doctors in that area. I called every friend I knew and asked for recommendations. We finally found a doctor who would operate at 6:30 p.m. I couldn't imagine the pain my mom was in, but she was a stalwart example to me.

My own pain level was intense, and all I wanted to do was crawl into bed with my mom. I called my sister in California and pleaded for help. She was on the plane the following morning. Mother was later moved to a rehabilitation center. My sister and I took turns: one with Mom and the other at home with Dad.

While coping with my own pain and caring for my parents, I often felt sustained from both sides of the veil. One dear friend drove me to radiation treatments then down to my parents' home, often towing along a grandchild. I was so overwhelmed with her love that I wept each day. I felt she had been sent by our loving Heavenly Father.

During this time while Mom was in rehab, my dad had a series of strokes. We arranged to bring Mom home for an afternoon so they could be together. Dad was sitting on the couch when we wheeled Mom in, and they both shed tears freely. They had been married seventy-two years, and for the first time in my life, I saw my mother cry, and it broke my heart.

A few days later, Dad slipped into a coma, and Mom sat by his bed and held his hand for hours. The next several days were an emotional roller coaster. Each morning during radiation treatment, I told myself I didn't have time for it, but as I went out the door, I'd see someone entering in much worse condition than I was. I told Heavenly Father I was sorry that I had been whining. The pace continued. I finished my radiation treatments and started daily chemotherapy.

Mother continued in rehab, but Dad did not come out of his coma. I was exhausted, hurting, and falling apart. Yet I became aware that Heavenly Father knew of my needs and was by my side each day.

My sister and I played music for our dad and talked to him constantly. Finally, the day came when we brought Mother to his side and lifted his head so she could have one last earthly kiss. My sister and I lay by his side for days until he quietly slipped away in the early morning hours.

I was totally drained, physically and emotionally, and now we had a funeral to plan. I had a terrible stress reaction to chemotherapy and broke out in a very painful rash all over my body. I had to put chemo off for a few weeks.

Dad's funeral plans proceeded well, but one thing seemed impossible. My father loved the Jim Reeves song "My Cathedral," but we couldn't find the sheet music anywhere, and no one even knew the song.

One morning a BYU music professor and friend of the family stopped at my brother's machine shop to get a window repaired, and that's when he learned of our father's death. He asked if there was anything he could do. My brother called me, and I told him we couldn't find anyone to sing "My Cathedral" at Dad's funeral. The professor said he had never heard of it but that he would download and listen to it. When my brother walked out to check the professor's car window, there was nothing wrong with it.

This musical artist figured out the music and played his guitar and sang this beautiful song at Dad's funeral. We felt that he had been brought to us as a gift of love from above.

For the next eighteen months, I continued on through several surgeries, heavy chemo, a pain pump implanted in my spinal column and hip, a bone-marrow transplant, and several abdominal reconstruction surgeries. I hallucinated on the morphine and had emergency life-saving procedures, bad reactions to transfusions and platelets, and experiences that I wouldn't wish on anyone. Many nights I lay in pain and thought the morning would never come. At those times, I thought about my pioneer ancestors sleeping on the hard, cold ground; burying loved ones along the way; and experiencing many other hard trials. They made it through hard times, and *so could I.* I visualized the many trials of Joseph Smith and those of our Savior, and I often wept at what they endured. I asked the Lord what He wanted me to learn from this experience, and I have had many answers.

Although I cannot reach remission with this cancer, I can get close. I am currently enjoying a respite before it returns, and I will have to repeat the chemo regimen again.

My husband has been an angel during these years. He moved his office home and tried to continue his business while taking care of me full time. When I couldn't sleep, Jack got up at all hours of the night to talk to me, pray with me, or rub my back. I was in bed for over two years, and he was right there with my home nurse, helping change my dressings. He gave me shots, helped me shower, prepared wonderful food for me, gave me blessings, and saw to my every request. I was in awe at the tender ways he always met my needs and never complained. He treated me like a queen, and I still weep when strangers say, "Oh, so you're Sandy! Your husband says your name with such reverence and has so much love for you."

Then there are the Relief Society presidents and their counselors. They quietly organized spiritual visits, service, and support activities. They didn't ask for attention or recognition, just lovingly served. I am indebted to them all.

Ward members have constantly come to our door to bring us wonderful meals; clean our home; share stories; mow our lawn; plant flowers; weed; take me to appointments; bring us treats; bottle fresh fruit; bring flowers, books, music, movies, and cookies; and even rub my numb feet and give us gingerbread houses at Christmas! The young men of the Aaronic priesthood have brought the sacrament to our home.

When I needed a little cheering up, cards often came by mail or quietly showed up at our door. Or someone special would call when I needed my spirits lifted. One night, when my immune system was completely wiped out by my bone-marrow transplant and I couldn't allow anyone into our home, members from our ward gathered outside my bedroom window and sang hymns to me. I still tear up whenever I think about that sweet event. I shall never forget it.

I was given an amazing priesthood blessing and was told that many spirits on the other side were pleading my case before the Lord. I believe that is why my life has been extended and Heavenly Father has granted me time to finish some important work I am doing, especially for those beyond the veil. That blessing has sustained me, and I am grateful to be alive. I am also grateful for those who keep me in their prayers and fast for me and for incredible priesthood blessings given by our bishop, our home teacher, our stake presidency, and my husband. I know with all my heart that Heavenly Father loves me and has sent many people to strengthen me in my time of need. He is very much aware of me, and I am so blessed to have so many Christlike people in my life.

Sandy Wallace and her husband, Jack, live in Sandy, Utah. They are the parents of two children and grandparents of four. They enjoy teaching and cooking with the International Dutch Oven Society, writing life histories and family cookbooks, working on genealogy, cooking, playing the piano, and spending time with family and friends. Before cancer, they enjoyed scuba diving, beachcombing, traveling, camping, and hiking—and hope to do them again.

I continue to gather stories that build faith, lift, and inspire others to believe in the promises of our Heavenly Father. If you have a story that you feel might help someone else, please contact me at judyedits@gmail.com or by going to my website at www.olseneditorial.com, which has writers' guidelines. I could not produce this series of books without the support of faithful Saints everywhere.

—Judy Olsen

About the Author

Judy C. Olsen has been writing and editing for LDS audiences for many years. She contributed stories and articles to the *Friend*, the *New Era*, and the *Church News* before working as an editor for the *Ensign* magazine.

After leaving the *Ensign*, Judy began writing books for Covenant, both fiction and nonfiction. She readily admits that this series of books about the watchcare we receive from our Heavenly Father throughout our lives has been a particular joy to compile. "I have grown close to and deeply admire many of those courageous souls who willingly share tender spiritual moments with us so that we might all be strengthened to move forward in faith."

Judy lives in Sandy, Utah, with her husband, Donald. They have four children and sixteen grandchildren.